CLASSIC RECIPES™

Publications International, Ltd.
Favorite Brand Name Recipes at www.fbnr.com

Microwave Cooking: Microwave ovens vary in wattage. Use the cooking times as
guidelines and check for doneness before adding more time.

Table of Contents

Down-Home Pies

Nothing makes pies so enticing as a tender, flaky Crisco® crust. Add a delicious filling and you have an unbeatable combination!

Chocolate Fudge Pie

CRUST

1 unbaked Classic CRISCO® Single Crust (page 36)

FILLING

1/4 CRISCO® Stick or 1/4 cup CRISCO® all-vegetable shortening

1 bar (4 ounces) sweet baking chocolate

1 can (14 ounces) sweetened condensed milk

1/2 cup all-purpose flour

2 eggs, beaten

1 teaspoon vanilla

1/4 teaspoon salt

1 cup flake coconut

1 cup chopped pecans

GARNISH

Unsweetened whipped cream or ice cream

1. For crust, prepare as directed. Do not bake. Heat oven to 350°F. Place wire rack on countertop for cooling pie.

2. For filling, melt 1/4 cup shortening and chocolate in heavy saucepan over low heat. Remove from heat. Stir in sweetened condensed milk, flour, eggs, vanilla and salt; mix well. Stir in coconut and nuts. Pour into unbaked pie crust.

3. Bake at 350°F for 40 minutes or until toothpick inserted into center comes out clean. Cool completely on wire rack.

4. Serve with unsweetened whipped cream or ice cream, if desired. Refrigerate leftover pie.   *Makes 1 (9-inch) pie (8 servings)*

Country Apple Rhubarb Pie

CRUST
>   1 unbaked Classic CRISCO® Double Crust (page 37)

FILLING
>   9 cups sliced peeled Granny Smith apples (about 3 pounds or
>   6 large apples)
> $1^1/_2$ cups fresh cut rhubarb ($^1/_2$-inch pieces), peeled if tough
> $^3/_4$ cup granulated sugar
> $^1/_2$ cup firmly packed light brown sugar
>   2 tablespoons all-purpose flour
>   1 tablespoon cornstarch
>   1 teaspoon ground cinnamon
> $^1/_4$ teaspoon freshly grated nutmeg

GLAZE
>   1 egg, beaten
>   1 tablespoon water
>   1 tablespoon granulated sugar
>   1 teaspoon ground pecans or walnuts
> $^1/_8$ teaspoon ground cinnamon

1. For crust, prepare as directed, using 9- or $9^1/_2$-inch deep-dish pie plate.
Do not bake. Heat oven to 425°F.

2. For filling, combine apples and rhubarb in large bowl. Combine $^3/_4$ cup
granulated sugar, brown sugar, flour, cornstarch, 1 teaspoon cinnamon and
nutmeg in medium bowl. Sprinkle over fruit. Toss to coat. Spoon into
unbaked pie crust. Moisten pastry edge with water. Cover pie with lattice
top, cutting strips $1^1/_4$ inches wide. Flute edge high.

3. For glaze, combine egg and water in small bowl. Brush over crust. Combine remaining glaze ingredients in another small bowl. Sprinkle over crust.

4. Bake at 425°F for 20 minutes. *Reduce oven temperature to 350°F.* Bake 30 to 40 minutes or until filling in center is bubbly and crust is golden brown. *Do not overbake.* Place sheet of foil or baking sheet under pie if it starts to bubble over. Cool to room temperature.

Makes 1 (9- or 9$^1/_2$-inch) deep-dish pie (8 servings)

Country Apple Rhubarb Pie

Classic Lemon Meringue Pie

CRUST

1 baked Classic CRISCO® Single Crust (page 36)

FILLING

1 1/2 cups granulated sugar

1/4 cup cornstarch

3 tablespoons all-purpose flour

1/4 teaspoon salt

1 1/2 cups hot water

3 egg yolks, beaten

2 tablespoons butter or margarine

1 1/2 teaspoons grated lemon peel

1/3 cup plus 1 tablespoon fresh lemon juice

MERINGUE

1/2 cup granulated sugar, divided

1 tablespoon cornstarch

1/2 cup cold water

4 egg whites

3/4 teaspoon vanilla

1. For crust, prepare and bake as directed. Cool. Heat oven to 350°F.

2. For filling, combine 1 1/2 cups sugar, 1/4 cup cornstarch, flour and salt in medium saucepan. Add 1 1/2 cups hot water gradually, stirring constantly. Cook and stir on medium heat until mixture comes to a boil and thickens. Reduce heat to low. Cook and stir constantly 8 minutes. Remove from heat. Add about one third of hot mixture slowly to egg yolks. Mix well. Return mixture to saucepan. Bring mixture to a boil on medium-high

heat. Reduce heat to low. Cook and stir 4 minutes. Remove from heat. Stir in butter and lemon peel. Add lemon juice slowly. Mix well. Spoon into baked pie crust.

3. For meringue, combine 2 tablespoons sugar, 1 tablespoon cornstarch and ¹/₂ cup cold water in small saucepan. Stir until cornstarch dissolves. Cook and stir on medium heat until mixture is clear. Cool.

4. Combine egg whites and vanilla in large bowl. Beat at high speed of electric mixer until soft peaks form. Beat in remaining 6 tablespoons sugar, 1 tablespoon at a time. Beat well after each addition. Combine meringue with cornstarch mixture and continue beating until stiff peaks form. Spread over filling, covering completely and sealing to edge of pie.

5. Bake at 350°F for 12 to 15 minutes or until meringue is golden. *Do not overbake.* Cool to room temperature before serving. Refrigerate leftover pie.   *Makes 1 (9-inch) pie (8 servings)*

Classic Lemon Meringue Pie

Peach Delight Pie

FILLING

   2$\frac{1}{2}$ cups sliced peeled peaches (about 1$\frac{1}{4}$ pounds or 2 to 3 large)

     $\frac{3}{4}$ cup granulated sugar

     $\frac{1}{4}$ cup quick-cooking tapioca

     1 teaspoon lemon juice

     1 teaspoon peach-flavored brandy

CRUMB MIXTURE

     $\frac{1}{4}$ cup all-purpose flour

     $\frac{1}{4}$ cup firmly packed light brown sugar

     $\frac{1}{4}$ cup chopped almonds

     3 tablespoons butter or margarine, melted

CRUST

     1 unbaked Classic CRISCO® Double Crust (page 37)

GLAZE

     1 egg white, lightly beaten

     Granulated sugar

1. For filling, combine peaches, $\frac{3}{4}$ cup granulated sugar, tapioca, lemon juice and brandy in medium bowl. Stir well. Let stand while making crumb mixture and crust.

2. For crumb mixture, combine flour, brown sugar, almonds and butter. Mix until crumbly.

3. For crust, prepare as directed. Do not bake. Heat oven to 425°F.

4. Sprinkle half of crumb mixture over unbaked pie crust. Add filling. Top with remaining crumb mixture. Cut out desired shapes from top crust with cookie cutter. Place on filling around edge of pie.

5. For glaze, brush cutouts with egg white. Sprinkle with granulated sugar. Cover edge of pie with foil to prevent overbrowning.

6. Bake at 425°F for 10 minutes. *Reduce oven temperature to 350°F. Bake 25 minutes. Do not overbake.* Remove foil. Bake 5 minutes. Serve warm or at room temperature. *Makes 1 (9-inch) pie (8 servings)*

Peach Delight Pie

Classic Pumpkin Pie with Candied Pecan Topping

CRUST

    1 unbaked Classic CRISCO® Single Crust (page 36)

FILLING

    1 can (16 ounces) solid-pack pumpkin (not pumpkin pie filling)

    1 can (12 ounces or $1^1/_2$ cups) evaporated milk

    2 eggs, beaten

    $^1/_2$ cup granulated sugar

    $^1/_4$ cup firmly packed light brown sugar

    1 teaspoon ground cinnamon

    $^1/_2$ teaspoon salt

    $^1/_2$ teaspoon ground ginger

    $^1/_4$ teaspoon ground nutmeg

    $^1/_8$ teaspoon ground cloves

TOPPING

    $^1/_4$ cup granulated sugar

    $^1/_4$ cup water

    2 tablespoons butter or margarine

    1 cup pecan pieces

1. For crust, prepare as directed using 9-inch glass pie dish. Do not bake. Heat oven to 350°F.

2. For filling, combine pumpkin, evaporated milk, eggs, $^1/_2$ cup granulated sugar, brown sugar, cinnamon, salt, ginger, nutmeg and cloves in large bowl. Mix well. Pour into unbaked pie crust.

3. Bake at 350°F for 1 hour 10 minutes or until knife inserted into center comes out clean. *Do not overbake.* Cool completely.

4. Grease baking sheet lightly with shortening.

5. For topping, combine ¼ cup granulated sugar and water in small saucepan. Cook and stir on medium heat until sugar dissolves. Increase heat. Bring to a boil. Boil 7 to 8 minutes or until mixture becomes light golden brown, stirring frequently. Stir in butter and nuts. Stir briskly. Spread quickly in thin layer on prepared baking sheet. Cool completely. Break into pieces. Sprinkle around edge of pie. (You might not use all of topping. Cover and store any extra for later use.) Refrigerate leftover pie.

Makes 1 (9-inch) pie (8 servings)

Classic Pumpkin Pie with Candied Pecan Topping

Crisco's® Door County Cherry Pie

FILLING

2 cans (16 ounces each) pitted red tart cherries in water

1 cup granulated sugar

$^1/_4$ cup cornstarch

1 cup reserved cherry liquid

CRUST

1 unbaked Classic CRISCO® Single Crust (page 36)

CREAM CHEESE LAYER

1 package (8 ounces) cream cheese, softened

$^1/_2$ cup granulated sugar

$^1/_2$ teaspoon vanilla

2 eggs

TOPPING

$1^1/_2$ cups dairy sour cream

1. For filling, drain cherries, reserving 1 cup liquid. Combine 1 cup sugar and cornstarch in medium saucepan. Stir in 3 cups cherries and 1 cup reserved liquid. Set aside remaining cherries for another use. Cook and stir on medium-high heat until mixture comes to a boil. Boil 1 minute. Cool while preparing crust.

2. For crust, prepare as directed. Do not bake. Heat oven to 425°F.

3. Spoon half of cherry filling into unbaked pie crust. Bake at 425°F for 15 minutes.

4. For cream cheese layer, beat cream cheese, $\frac{1}{2}$ cup sugar and vanilla in small bowl at medium speed of electric mixer until smooth. Beat in eggs until blended. Spoon cream cheese mixture over cherry filling.

5. *Reduce oven temperature to 350°F.* Return pie to oven. Bake 25 minutes. *Do not overbake.* Cool to room temperature. Top with remaining cherry mixture.

6. For topping, place spoonfuls of sour cream around edge of pie. Refrigerate leftover pie.   *Makes 1 (9-inch) pie (8 servings)*

Crisco's® Door County Cherry Pie

Delaware Blueberry Pie

CRUST
>   1 unbaked Classic CRISCO® Double Crust (page 37)

FILLING
> $4^1/_2$ cups fresh blueberries, divided
> $^1/_2$ cup granulated sugar
> $^1/_2$ cup firmly packed light brown sugar
>   2 tablespoons plus $1^1/_2$ teaspoons cornstarch
> $^1/_2$ teaspoon ground cinnamon
> $^1/_8$ teaspoon salt
>   1 tablespoon butter or margarine
>   1 teaspoon peach schnapps
>   2 tablespoons quick-cooking tapioca
>   4 to 5 drops red food coloring (optional)

DECORATIONS
>   Reserved dough
>   2 tablespoons melted vanilla frozen yogurt

1. For crust, prepare as directed, reserving dough scraps for decorations, if desired. Do not bake. Heat oven to 425°F.

2. For filling, place $^1/_2$ cup blueberries in resealable plastic sandwich bag. Crush berries. Pour juice and berries into strainer over liquid measuring cup. Press berries to extract all juice. Pour water over berries until juice measures $^1/_2$ cup.

3. Combine sugars, cornstarch, cinnamon and salt in large saucepan. Add blueberry juice mixture. Cook and stir on medium heat until mixture boils. Remove from heat. Stir in butter and schnapps. Set pan in cold

water about 5 minutes to cool. Stir in tapioca. Add food coloring, if desired. Carefully stir in remaining 4 cups blueberries. Spoon into unbaked pie crust. Moisten pastry edge with water.

4. Cover pie with top crust. Fold top edge under bottom crust; flute with fingers or fork.

5. For decorations, cut stars and diamonds from reserved dough. Dip cutouts in melted frozen yogurt. Place on top of pie and around edge. Cut slits in top crust to allow steam to escape.

6. Bake at 425°F for 15 minutes. Cover cutouts and edge of pie with foil, if necessary, to prevent overbrowning. *Reduce oven temperature to 375°F.* Bake 20 to 25 minutes or until filling in center is bubbly and crust is golden brown. *Do not overbake.* Cool to room temperature before serving.   *Makes 1 (9-inch) pie (8 servings)*

Delaware Blueberry Pie

Pennsylvania Shoo-Fly Pie

CRUST

  1 unbaked Classic CRISCO® Single Crust (page 36)

CRUMB MIXTURE

  2 cups all-purpose flour

  $1/2$ cup firmly packed light brown sugar

  $1/3$ cup butter or margarine, softened

LIQUID MIXTURE

  1 cup boiling water

  1 teaspoon baking soda

  $3/4$ cup plus 2 tablespoons dark molasses

  2 tablespoons light molasses

1. For crust, prepare as directed. Do not bake. Heat oven to 375°F.

2. For crumb mixture, combine flour, brown sugar and butter in bowl. Mix until fine crumbs form. Reserve $1/2$ cup for topping.

3. For liquid mixture, combine water and baking soda in large bowl. Stir until foamy. Add dark and light molasses. Stir well until foamy. Pour into unbaked pie crust. Add crumb mixture. Stir gently until mixed. Sprinkle reserved $1/2$ cup crumbs on top. Bake at 375°F for 45 to 55 minutes or until set. *Do not overbake.* Cool until warm or room temperature before serving.   *Makes 1 (9-inch) pie (8 servings)*

Pennsylvania Shoo-Fly Pie

Sumptuous Strawberry Rhubarb Pie

CRUST

    1 unbaked Classic CRISCO® Double Crust (page 37)

FILLING

    4 cups fresh cut rhubarb ($1/2$-inch pieces), peeled if tough

    3 cups sliced strawberries

    $1^1/3$ cups granulated sugar

    $1/3$ cup plus $1/4$ cup all-purpose flour

    2 tablespoons plus $1^1/2$ teaspoons quick-cooking tapioca

    $1/2$ teaspoon grated orange peel

    $1/2$ teaspoon ground cinnamon

    $1/4$ teaspoon ground nutmeg

    2 tablespoons butter or margarine

GLAZE

    1 egg, beaten

    1 tablespoon granulated sugar

1. For crust, prepare as directed. Do not bake. Heat oven to 425°F.

2. For filling, combine rhubarb and strawberries in large bowl. Combine $1^1/3$ cups sugar, flour, tapioca, orange peel, cinnamon and nutmeg in medium bowl; stir well. Add to fruit. Toss to coat. Spoon filling into unbaked pie crust. Dot with butter. Moisten pastry edge with water.

3. Roll out top crust. Lift onto filled pie. Trim $1/2$ inch beyond edge of pie plate. Fold top edge under bottom crust; flute. Cut desired shapes into top crust to allow steam to escape.

4. For glaze, brush top crust with egg. Sprinkle with 1 tablespoon sugar.

5. Bake at 425°F for 40 to 50 minutes or until filling in center is bubbly and crust is golden brown. *Do not overbake.* Cover edge with foil, if necessary, to prevent overbrowning. Cool until barely warm or room temperature before serving.   *Makes 1 (9-inch) pie (8 servings)*

Sumptuous Strawberry Rhubarb Pie

Double Blueberry Cheese Pie

CRUST

    1 unbaked Classic CRISCO® Single Crust (page 36)

FILLING

    2 packages (8 ounces each) cream cheese, softened

    1 cup granulated sugar

    2 tablespoons all-purpose flour

    2 eggs

    2 teaspoons vanilla

    $^1/_2$ cup whipping cream

    2 cups fresh blueberries

TOPPING

    2 cups whipping cream

    2 tablespoons confectioners' sugar

    1 teaspoon vanilla

    1 cup fresh blueberries

1. For crust, prepare as directed using 9- or $9^1/_2$-inch deep-dish pie plate. Do not bake. Heat oven to 350°F.

2. For filling, place cream cheese and granulated sugar in food processor bowl. Process, using steel blade, until smooth. Add flour, eggs, 2 teaspoons vanilla and $^1/_2$ cup whipping cream through feed tube while processor is running. Process until blended. Add 2 cups blueberries. Pulse (quick on and off) twice. Pour into unbaked pie crust.

3. Bake at 350°F for 45 minutes. *Do not overbake.* Turn oven off. Allow pie to remain in oven with door ajar for 1 hour. Cool to room temperature. Refrigerate 6 hours or overnight.

4. For topping, beat 2 cups whipping cream in large bowl at high speed of electric mixer until stiff peaks form. Beat in confectioners' sugar and 1 teaspoon vanilla. Spread over top of pie. Garnish with 1 cup blueberries. Serve immediately. Refrigerate leftover pie.

Makes 1 (9- or 9½-inch) deep-dish pie (8 servings)

Double Blueberry Cheese Pie

Lemon Chiffon Cloud Pie

CRUST
   1 baked Classic CRISCO® Single Crust (page 36)

FILLING
   $^3/_4$ cup granulated sugar
   1 envelope unflavored gelatin
   $^1/_4$ teaspoon salt
   1 cup water
   $^1/_3$ cup strained fresh lemon juice
   2 egg yolks, beaten
   $1^1/_2$ teaspoons grated lemon peel
   $1^1/_2$ cups thawed frozen whipped topping

GARNISH
   $^1/_2$ cup or more thawed frozen whipped topping
      Thin strips of fresh lemon peel
      Fresh lemon slices
      Mint leaves

1. For crust, prepare and bake as directed. Cool completely.

2. For filling, combine sugar, gelatin and salt in medium saucepan. Add water, lemon juice and egg yolks. Stir until well blended. Cook and stir on medium heat about 5 minutes or until gelatin is dissolved. Remove from heat. Stir in grated lemon peel. Transfer to medium bowl. Refrigerate until thickened.

3. Place bowl of filling in larger bowl containing ice and water. Beat at high speed of electric mixer 7 to 10 minutes or until double in volume.

Fold in 1 1/2 cups whipped topping. Spoon into cooled baked pie crust. Refrigerate at least 2 hours before serving.

4. For garnish, spoon 1/2 cup whipped topping into decorator bag fitted with large star tip. Pipe rosettes around edge of pie. Place lemon peel strips between rosettes. Pipe one large rosette in center of pie. Garnish with twisted lemon slices and mint leaves. Refrigerate leftovers.

Makes 1 (9-inch) pie (8 servings)

Note: Prepare Classic Crisco® Double Crust (page 37), if desired. Save half to make leaf cutouts to decorate edge of pie.

Lemon Chiffon Cloud Pie

Cider Apple Pie in Cheddar Crust

CRUST
> 2 cups sifted all-purpose flour
> 1 cup shredded Cheddar cheese
> $1/2$ teaspoon salt
> $2/3$ CRISCO® Stick or $2/3$ cup CRISCO® all-vegetable shortening
> 5 to 6 tablespoons ice water

FILLING
> 6 cups sliced peeled apples (about 2 pounds or 6 medium)
> 1 cup apple cider
> $2/3$ cup granulated sugar
> 2 tablespoons cornstarch
> 2 tablespoons water
> $1/2$ teaspoon ground cinnamon
> 1 tablespoon butter or margarine

GLAZE
> 1 egg yolk
> 1 tablespoon water

1. Heat oven to 400°F.

2. For crust, place flour, cheese and salt in food processor bowl. Add $2/3$ cup shortening. Process 15 seconds. Sprinkle water through feed tube, 1 tablespoon at a time, just until dough forms (process time not to exceed 20 seconds). Shape into ball. Divide dough in half. Press between hands to form two 5- to 6-inch "pancakes." Roll and press bottom crust into 9-inch pie plate.

3. For filling, combine apples, apple cider and sugar in large saucepan. Cook and stir on medium-high heat until mixture comes to a boil. Reduce heat to

low. Simmer 5 minutes. Combine cornstarch, water and cinnamon. Stir into apples. Cook and stir until mixture comes to a boil. Remove from heat. Stir in butter. Spoon into unbaked pie crust. Moisten pastry edge with water.

4. Roll top crust. Lift onto filled pie. Trim $1/2$ inch beyond edge of pie plate. Fold top edge under bottom crust. Flute. Cut slits or design in top crust to allow steam to escape.

5. For glaze, beat egg yolk with fork. Stir in water. Brush over top.

6. Bake at 400°F for 35 to 40 minutes or until filling in center is bubbly and crust is golden brown. Cover edge with foil, if necessary, to prevent overbrowning. *Do not overbake.* Cool to room temperature before serving.

Makes 1 (9-inch) pie (8 servings)

Note: Golden Delicious, Granny Smith and Jonathan apples are all suitable for pie baking.

Cider Apple Pie in Cheddar Crust

Mixed Berry Pie

CRUST
   1 unbaked Classic CRISCO® Double Crust (page 37)

FILLING
   2 cups canned or frozen blackberries, thawed and well drained
   1 1/2 cups canned or frozen blueberries, thawed and well drained
   1/2 cup canned or frozen gooseberries, thawed and well drained
   1/8 teaspoon almond extract
   1/4 cup granulated sugar
   3 tablespoons cornstarch

1. For crust, prepare as directed. Do not bake. Heat oven to 425°F.

2. For filling, combine blackberries, blueberries, gooseberries and almond extract in large bowl. Combine sugar and cornstarch. Add to berries. Toss well to mix. Spoon into unbaked pie crust.

3. Cut top crust into leaf shapes and arrange on top of pie, or cover pie with top crust. Flute edge. Cut slits into top crust, if using, to allow steam to escape.

4. Bake at 425°F for 40 minutes or until filling in center is bubbly and crust is golden brown. *Do not overbake.* Cool until barely warm or room temperature before serving.   *Makes 1 (9-inch) pie (8 servings)*

Mixed Berry Pie

Peanut Cream Surprise Pie

CRUST
> 1 baked Classic CRISCO® Single Crust (page 36)

CHOCOLATE LAYER
> 1 package (6 ounces) semisweet chocolate chips (1 cup)
> 2 tablespoons CRISCO® Stick or 2 tablespoons CRISCO®
>   all-vegetable shortening

FILLING
> 2½ cups milk
> 1 cup peanut butter chips
> ½ cup firmly packed light brown sugar
> ⅓ cup all-purpose flour
> ¼ teaspoon salt
> 3 egg yolks, beaten
> 3 tablespoons unsalted butter or margarine
> 1 teaspoon vanilla
> 1 cup chopped peanuts

TOPPING
> ¼ cup semisweet chocolate chips
> 1½ teaspoons CRISCO® Stick or 1½ teaspoons CRISCO®
>   all-vegetable shortening

1. For crust, prepare and bake as directed. Cool.

2. For chocolate layer, combine 1 cup chocolate chips and 2 tablespoons shortening in microwave-safe bowl. Microwave at 50% (MEDIUM) 2 to 3 minutes or until melted, stirring after each minute. Stir until smooth. Pour over bottom of cooled baked pie crust.

3. For filling, combine milk, peanut butter chips, brown sugar, flour and salt in medium saucepan. Cook and stir on medium heat until mixture boils and thickens. Cook and stir 2 more minutes. Remove from heat.

4. Add 1 cup hot filling slowly to egg yolks, stirring constantly. Return to saucepan. Cook and stir 2 minutes. Remove from heat. Add butter and vanilla; stir until butter melts. Pour over chocolate layer in pie crust. Sprinkle with nuts.

5. For topping, combine ¼ cup chocolate chips and 1½ teaspoons shortening in microwave-safe cup. Microwave at 50% (MEDIUM) 1 to 2 minutes or until melted, stirring after each minute. Stir until smooth. Drizzle over nuts. Cover top with waxed paper. Refrigerate until set.

Makes 1 (9-inch) pie (8 servings)

Peanut Cream Surprise Pie

Golden Ambrosia Pecan Pie

CRUST

    1 unbaked Classic CRISCO® Single Crust (page 36)

FILLING

    3 eggs, beaten

    $3/4$ cup light corn syrup

    $1/2$ cup granulated sugar

    3 tablespoons firmly packed light brown sugar

    2 tablespoons butter or margarine, melted

    3 tablespoons thawed frozen orange juice concentrate

    2 tablespoons cornstarch

    1 teaspoon grated orange peel

    1 teaspoon vanilla

    $1/2$ teaspoon coconut extract or flavor

  $1 1/2$ cups chopped pecans

    $2/3$ cup flake coconut

1. For crust, prepare as directed. Do not bake. Heat oven to 350°F.

2. For filling, combine eggs, corn syrup, sugars and butter in large bowl. Stir well. Combine orange juice concentrate, cornstarch, orange peel, vanilla and coconut extract. Add to egg mixture. Stir well. Stir in nuts and coconut. Pour into unbaked pie crust. Cover edge with foil to prevent overbrowning.

3. Bake at 350°F for 35 minutes. Remove foil. Bake for 15 to 20 minutes or until set and crust is golden brown. *Do not overbake.* Cool to room temperature before serving. Garnish as desired.

Makes 1 (9-inch) pie (8 servings)

Golden Ambrosia Pecan Pie

Classic Crisco® Single Crust

1¹/₃ cups all-purpose flour
¹/₂ teaspoon salt
¹/₂ CRISCO® Stick or ¹/₂ cup CRISCO® all-vegetable shortening
3 tablespoons cold water

1. Spoon flour into measuring cup and level. Combine flour and salt in medium bowl.

2. Cut in ¹/₂ cup shortening using pastry blender or 2 knives until all flour is blended to form pea-size chunks.

3. Sprinkle with water, 1 tablespoon at a time. Toss lightly with fork until dough forms a ball.

4. Press dough between hands to form 5- to 6-inch "pancake." Flour rolling surface and rolling pin lightly. Roll dough into circle. Trim circle 1 inch larger than upside-down pie plate. Carefully remove trimmed dough. Set aside to reroll and use for pastry cutout garnish, if desired.

5. Fold dough into quarters. Unfold and press into 9-inch pie plate. Fold edge under. Flute.

6. **For recipes using a baked pie crust,** heat oven to 425°F. Prick bottom and side thoroughly with fork (50 times) to prevent shrinkage. Bake at 425°F for 10 to 15 minutes or until lightly browned.

7. **For recipes using an unbaked pie crust,** follow directions given for that recipe.   *Makes 1 (9-inch) single crust*

Classic Crisco® Double Crust

2 cups all-purpose flour
1 teaspoon salt
¾ CRISCO® Stick or ¾ cup CRISCO® all-vegetable shortening
5 tablespoons cold water (or more as needed)

1. Spoon flour into measuring cup and level. Combine flour and salt in medium bowl.

2. Cut in ¾ cup shortening using pastry blender or 2 knives until all flour is blended to form pea-size chunks.

3. Sprinkle with water, 1 tablespoon at a time. Toss lightly with fork until dough forms a ball. Divide dough in half.

4. Press dough between hands to form two 5- to 6-inch "pancakes." Flour rolling surface and rolling pin lightly. Roll both halves of dough into circle. Trim one circle of dough 1 inch larger than upside-down pie plate. Carefully remove trimmed dough. Set aside to reroll and use for pastry cutout garnish, if desired.

5. Fold dough into quarters. Unfold and press into 9-inch pie plate. Trim edge even with plate. Add desired filling to unbaked crust. Moisten pastry edge with water. Lift top crust onto filled pie. Trim ½ inch beyond edge of pie plate. Fold top edge under bottom crust. Flute. Cut slits in top crust to allow steam to escape. Follow baking directions given for that recipe.

Makes 1 (9-inch) double crust

Old-Fashioned Cakes

Birthdays and special occasions wouldn't be the same without a beautiful cake. These favorites will have the whole gang celebrating just because you baked!

Chocolate Raspberry Avalanche Cake

2 cups all-purpose flour

2 cups granulated sugar

6 tablespoons unsweetened cocoa powder

1 1/2 teaspoons baking soda

1 teaspoon salt

1 cup hot coffee

3/4 Butter Flavor CRISCO® Stick or 3/4 cup Butter Flavor CRISCO®
   all-vegetable shortening plus additional for greasing

1/2 cup milk

3 eggs

1/4 cup raspberry-flavored liqueur

Confectioners' sugar

1 cup fresh raspberries

1. Heat oven to 350°F. Grease 10-inch (12-cup) Bundt pan with shortening. Flour lightly. Place wire rack on countertop for cooling cake.

2. Combine flour, granulated sugar, cocoa, baking soda and salt in large bowl. Add coffee and 3/4 cup shortening. Beat at low speed of electric mixer until dry ingredients are moistened. Add milk. Beat at medium speed 1 1/2 minutes. Add eggs, 1 at a time, beating well after each addition. Pour into prepared pan.

3. Bake at 350°F for 40 to 45 minutes or until toothpick inserted near center comes out clean. *Do not overbake.* Cool 10 minutes before removing from pan. Place cake, fluted side up, on wire rack. Cool 10 minutes. Brush top and side with liqueur. Cool completely. Dust with confectioners' sugar.

4. Place cake on serving plate. Fill center with raspberries.

Makes 1 (10-inch) cake (12 to 16 servings)

Arlington Apple Gingerbread Cake

CAKE

    2 cans (20 ounces each) sliced apples, drained

    1 cup plus 1 teaspoon granulated sugar, divided

    2 teaspoons ground cinnamon, divided

    2 teaspoons fresh lemon juice

    1 teaspoon grated lemon peel

    $^1/_2$ Butter Flavor CRISCO® Stick or $^1/_2$ cup Butter Flavor
        CRISCO® all-vegetable shortening

    1 cup light molasses

    2 eggs

    3 cups all-purpose flour

    2 teaspoons ground ginger

    $^1/_2$ teaspoon ground cloves

    1 cup boiling water

    2 teaspoons baking soda

TOPPING (OPTIONAL)

    Confectioners' sugar

    Prepared lemon pie filling

    Whipped cream

1. Heat oven to 350°F. Place wire rack on countertop for cooling cake.

2. For cake, arrange apple slices in bottom of ungreased 13×9×2-inch baking pan. Combine 1 teaspoon granulated sugar and 1 teaspoon cinnamon in small bowl. Sprinkle over apples along with lemon juice and lemon peel.

3. Combine $^1/_2$ cup shortening and remaining 1 cup granulated sugar in large bowl. Beat until blended. Add molasses and eggs. Beat until blended.

4. Combine flour, ginger, remaining 1 teaspoon cinnamon and cloves in medium bowl. Add to molasses mixture. Beat until blended.

5. Combine boiling water and baking soda. Stir into molasses mixture until blended. Pour over apple mixture.

6. Bake at 350°F for 50 to 60 minutes or until toothpick inserted into center comes out clean. *Do not overbake.* Cool completely in pan on wire rack.

7. For optional topping, sprinkle top of cake with confectioners' sugar. Place spoonfuls of pie filling and whipped cream on each serving.

Makes 1 (13×9×2-inch) cake (12 to 16 servings)

Arlington Apple Gingerbread Cake

Sour Cream Bundt Cake

CINNAMON−SUGAR

    6 tablespoons granulated sugar

    2 tablespoons ground cinnamon

CAKE

    $2^3/_4$ cups all-purpose flour

    1 cup granulated sugar

    1 package (4-serving size) vanilla flavor instant pudding and pie filling mix (not sugar-free)

    1 tablespoon plus 1 teaspoon baking powder

    $^1/_2$ teaspoon salt

    1 cup (8 ounces) dairy sour cream

    $^3/_4$ CRISCO® Stick or $^3/_4$ cup CRISCO® all-vegetable shortening

    $^3/_4$ cup milk

    4 eggs

    2 teaspoons vanilla

    Reserved cinnamon sugar

1. Heat oven to 350°F. Grease 10-inch (12-cup) Bundt pan. Place wire rack on countertop for cooling cake.

2. For cinnamon-sugar, combine 6 tablespoons sugar and cinnamon in small bowl. Sprinkle in pan until generously coated. Reserve remaining cinnamon-sugar.

3. For cake, combine flour, 1 cup sugar, pudding mix, baking powder and salt in large bowl. Beat at low speed of electric mixer. Add sour cream, $^3/_4$ cup shortening, milk, eggs and vanilla. Beat at medium speed 1 minute. Pour half of batter (about 3 cups) into prepared pan. Sprinkle with reserved cinnamon-sugar. Cover with remaining batter.

4. Bake at 350°F for 1 hour to 1 hour 10 minutes or until toothpick inserted near center comes out clean. *Do not overbake.* Cool 20 minutes on wire rack before removing from pan. Place cake, fluted side up, on serving plate. Serve warm or at room temperature.

Makes 1 (10-inch) bundt cake (12 to 16 servings)

Pineapple-Coconut Party Cake

CAKE

    2 cups granulated sugar

    1 Butter Flavor CRISCO® Stick or 1 cup Butter Flavor CRISCO®
        all-vegetable shortening plus additional for greasing

    3 eggs

    1 teaspoon vanilla

    1 teaspoon coconut extract

    3 cups sifted all-purpose flour

    1 tablespoon baking powder

    1 cup milk

TOPPING

    1 can (20 ounces) crushed pineapple or pineapple tidbits in
        unsweetened juice, undrained

    1 tablespoon cornstarch

    1 cup firmly packed light brown sugar

    1 cup shredded coconut

    1 cup chopped pecans

    $1/2$ teaspoon rum extract

    $1/4$ teaspoon vanilla

    12 to 16 maraschino cherries, drained

continued on page 44

Pineapple-Coconut Party Cake, continued

1. Heat oven to 350°F. Grease 13×9×2-inch baking pan with shortening. Flour lightly. Place wire rack on countertop for cooling cake.

2. For cake, combine granulated sugar and 1 cup shortening in large bowl. Beat at medium speed of electric mixer until light and fluffy. Add eggs, 1 at a time, beating well after each addition. Beat in 1 teaspoon vanilla and coconut extract until blended.

3. Combine flour and baking powder in medium bowl. Add to creamed mixture alternately with milk, beating at low speed after each addition until well blended. Beat at medium speed 2 minutes. Pour into prepared pan. Spread evenly. (Batter will be very thick.)

4. Bake at 350°F for 35 to 45 minutes or until toothpick inserted into center comes out clean. *Do not overbake.* (Cake will rise above top of pan and then fall slightly. Cake may be slightly lower in center.) Cool completely in pan on wire rack.

5. For topping, combine 2 tablespoons juice from pineapple and cornstarch in small bowl. Stir to dissolve.

6. Combine pineapple, remaining juice and brown sugar in medium saucepan. Bring to a boil. Stir in cornstarch mixture. Boil and stir 1 minute or until mixture is thickened and clear. Remove from heat. Stir in coconut, nuts, rum extract and $1/4$ teaspoon vanilla.

7. Use large fork or skewer to poke holes in top of cake. Pour topping over cake, spreading to edges. Arrange cherries on top of cake so that when cake is cut, each slice will have cherry in center. Refrigerate at least 30 minutes before serving.

Makes 1 (13×9×2-inch) cake (12 to 16 servings)

Note: Prepare cake and topping the day before serving, if desired.

Pineapple-Coconut Party Cake

Magnificent Pound Cake

CAKE

    3 cups granulated sugar

    1 Butter Flavor CRISCO® Stick or 1 cup Butter Flavor
        CRISCO® all-vegetable shortening plus additional for
        greasing

    5 eggs

  $3^1/_3$ cups all-purpose flour

    $^1/_2$ teaspoon baking powder

    $^1/_2$ teaspoon salt

    1 cup milk

    1 teaspoon coconut extract

    1 teaspoon rum extract

GLAZE

    $^1/_2$ cup granulated sugar

    $^1/_4$ cup water

    $^1/_2$ teaspoon pure almond extract

GARNISH (OPTIONAL)

    Assorted fresh fruit

1. Heat oven to 325°F. Grease 10-inch (12-cup) Bundt pan. Flour lightly. Place wire rack on countertop for cooling cake.

2. For cake, mix 3 cups sugar and 1 cup shortening. Beat at low speed of electric mixer until blended. Beat at medium speed until well blended. Add eggs, 1 at a time, beating 1 minute at low speed after each addition.

3. Combine flour, baking powder and salt in medium bowl. Add to creamed mixture alternately with milk, beginning and ending with flour

mixture, beating at low speed after each addition until well blended. Add coconut extract and rum extract. Beat at medium speed 1 minute. Pour into prepared pan.

4. Bake at 325°F for 1 hour 30 minutes to 1 hour 40 minutes or until toothpick inserted near center comes out clean. *Do not overbake.* Cool 10 minutes before removing from pan. Place cake, fluted side up, on wire rack. Cool 20 minutes.

5. For glaze, combine ½ cup sugar, water and almond extract in small saucepan. Bring to a boil. Slide waxed paper under wire rack. Brush glaze over warm cake, using all of glaze. Cool completely.

6. For optional garnish, place spoonful of assorted fresh fruit on each serving.   *Makes 1 (10-inch) bundt cake (12 to 16 servings)*

Magnificent Pound Cake

Glazed Chocolate Pound Cake

CAKE

 1³/₄ Butter Flavor CRISCO® Sticks or 1³/₄ cups Butter Flavor
   CRISCO® all-vegetable shortening plus additional for
   greasing

  3 cups granulated sugar

  5 eggs

  1 teaspoon vanilla

 3¹/₄ cups all-purpose flour

  ¹/₂ cup unsweetened cocoa powder

  1 teaspoon baking powder

  ¹/₂ teaspoon salt

 1¹/₃ cups milk

  1 cup miniature semisweet chocolate chips

GLAZE

  1 cup miniature semisweet chocolate chips

  ¹/₄ Butter Flavor CRISCO® Stick or ¹/₄ cup Butter Flavor
   CRISCO® all-vegetable shortening

  1 tablespoon light corn syrup

1. For cake, heat oven to 325°F. Grease and flour 10-inch tube pan.
Place wire rack on countertop for cooling cake.

2. Combine 1³/₄ cups shortening, sugar, eggs and vanilla in large bowl.
Beat at low speed of electric mixer until blended, scraping bowl frequently.
Beat at high speed 6 minutes, scraping bowl occasionally. Combine flour,
cocoa, baking powder and salt in medium bowl. Mix in dry ingredients
alternately with milk, beating after each addition until batter is smooth.
Stir in 1 cup chocolate chips. Spoon into prepared pan.

3. Bake at 325°F for 75 to 85 minutes or until toothpick inserted near center comes out clean. Cool on wire rack 20 minutes. Invert onto serving dish. Cool completely.

4. For glaze, combine 1 cup chocolate chips, ¼ cup shortening and corn syrup in top part of double boiler over hot, not boiling, water. Stir just until melted and smooth. Cool slightly. (Or place mixture in microwave-safe bowl. Microwave at 50% (Medium) power for 1 minute and 15 seconds. Stir. Repeat at 15-second intervals, if necessary, just until melted and smooth. Cool slightly.) Spoon glaze over cake. Let stand until glaze is firm.

Makes 1 (10-inch) tube cake

Glazed Chocolate Pound Cake

Coconut Pound Cake

CAKE

2 cups granulated sugar

1 Butter Flavor CRISCO® Stick or 1 cup Butter Flavor CRISCO®
all-vegetable shortening plus additional for greasing

5 eggs

1$\frac{1}{2}$ teaspoons coconut extract

2$\frac{1}{4}$ cups all-purpose flour

1$\frac{1}{2}$ teaspoons baking powder

$\frac{1}{2}$ teaspoon salt

1 cup buttermilk or sour milk*

1 cup shredded coconut, chopped

GLAZE

$\frac{1}{2}$ cup granulated sugar

$\frac{1}{4}$ cup water

1$\frac{1}{2}$ teaspoons coconut extract

GARNISH (OPTIONAL)

Whipped topping or whipped cream

Assorted fresh fruit

*To sour milk: Combine 1 tablespoon white vinegar plus enough milk to equal 1 cup. Stir. Wait 5 minutes before using.

1. Heat oven to 350°F. Grease 10-inch tube pan with shortening. Flour lightly. Place wire rack on countertop to cool cake.

2. For cake, combine 2 cups sugar and 1 cup shortening in large bowl. Beat at medium speed of electric mixer until blended. Add eggs, 1 at a time, beating after each addition. Beat in 1$\frac{1}{2}$ teaspoons coconut extract.

3. Combine flour, baking powder and salt in medium bowl. Add alternately with buttermilk to creamed mixture, beating at low speed after each addition until well blended. Add coconut. Mix until blended. Spoon into prepared pan.

4. Bake at 350°F for 50 minutes or until toothpick inserted near center comes out clean. *Do not overbake.* Remove to wire rack. Cool 5 minutes. Remove cake from pan. Place cake, top side up, on serving plate. Use toothpick to poke 12 to 15 holes in top of cake.

5. For glaze, combine $^1/_2$ cup sugar, water and $1^1/_2$ teaspoons coconut extract in small saucepan. Cook and stir over medium heat until mixture comes to a boil. Remove from heat. Cool 15 minutes. Spoon over cake. Cool completely.

6. For optional garnish, place spoonfuls of whipped topping and assorted fresh fruit on each serving.

Makes 1 (10-inch) tube cake (12 to 16 servings)

Coconut Pound Cake

Pumpkin Cake with Orange Glaze

CAKE

>   2 cups firmly packed light brown sugar
>   3/4 Butter Flavor CRISCO® Stick or 3/4 cup Butter Flavor
>   CRISCO® all-vegetable shortening plus additional for
>   greasing
>   4 eggs
>   1 can (16 ounces) solid-pack pumpkin (not pumpkin pie filling)
>   1/4 cup water
>   2 1/2 cups cake flour
>   1 tablespoon plus 1 teaspoon baking powder
>   1 tablespoon pumpkin pie spice
>   1 1/2 teaspoons baking soda
>   1 teaspoon salt
>   1/2 cup chopped walnuts
>   1/2 cup raisins

GLAZE

>   1 cup confectioners' sugar
>   1 tablespoon plus 1 teaspoon orange juice
>   3/4 teaspoon grated orange peel
>   Additional chopped walnuts

1. Heat oven to 350°F. Grease 10-inch (12-cup) Bundt pan. Flour lightly.

2. For cake, combine brown sugar and 3/4 cup shortening in large bowl. Beat at low speed with electric mixer until creamy. Add eggs, 1 at a time, beating well after each addition. Stir in pumpkin and water.

3. Combine flour, baking powder, pumpkin pie spice, baking soda and salt in medium bowl. Add to pumpkin mixture. Beat at low speed with electric

mixer until blended. Beat 2 minutes at medium speed. Fold in $1/2$ cup nuts and raisins. Spoon into prepared pan.

4. Bake at 350°F for 55 to 60 minutes or until toothpick inserted near center comes out clean. Cool 10 minutes before removing from pan. Place cake, fluted side up, on serving plate. Cool completely.

5. For glaze, combine confectioners' sugar, orange juice and orange peel in small bowl. Stir with spoon to blend. Spoon over top of cake, letting excess glaze run down side. Sprinkle with additional nuts before glaze hardens. *Makes 1 (10-inch) bundt cake (12 to 16 servings)*

Pumpkin Cake with Orange Glaze

Orange Poppy Seed Cake

CAKE

2 medium navel oranges

1 1/4 cups milk

2 2/3 cups cake flour

2 tablespoons poppy seeds

1 teaspoon baking soda

3/4 teaspoon salt

2 cups granulated sugar

3/4 Butter Flavor CRISCO® Stick or 3/4 cup Butter Flavor
    CRISCO® all-vegetable shortening plus additional for
    greasing

3 eggs

1/2 teaspoon vanilla

FROSTING

1 package (8 ounces) cream cheese, softened

1/3 stick plus 1 tablespoon Butter Flavor Crisco® Stick or 1/3 cup
    plus 1 tablespoon Butter Flavor Crisco® all-vegetable
    shortening

Reserved orange pulp

1 teaspoon reserved grated orange peel

1/8 teaspoon salt

3 cups confectioners' sugar

Reserved 1/4 teaspoon orange juice

1. Heat oven to 350°F. Grease 13×9×2-inch baking pan. Flour lightly.
Place wire rack on countertop for cooling cake.

2. For cake, grate enough peel from oranges to yield 1 tablespoon plus 2 teaspoons. Reserve 1 teaspoon for frosting. Squeeze oranges to yield ¼ cup plus ¼ teaspoon orange juice. Scrape any extra pulp from oranges. Reserve pulp and ¼ teaspoon juice for frosting. Combine ¼ cup juice and milk in small bowl.

3. Combine flour, poppy seeds, baking soda and ¾ teaspoon salt in medium bowl.

4. Combine granulated sugar, ¾ cup shortening and 1 tablespoon plus 1 teaspoon grated orange peel in large bowl. Beat at medium speed of electric mixer 5 minutes or until well blended. Beat in eggs, 1 at a time, beating well after each addition. Add vanilla. Beat until blended.

5. Reduce speed to low. Add flour mixture in thirds alternately with milk mixture, beating after each addition just until smooth. Pour into prepared pan.

6. Bake at 350°F for 25 to 35 minutes or until toothpick inserted into center comes out clean. Cool completely in pan on wire rack. Place cake on serving plate.

7. For frosting, combine cream cheese, ⅓ cup plus 1 tablespoon shortening, reserved orange pulp, reserved 1 teaspoon grated orange peel and ⅛ teaspoon salt in large bowl. Beat at medium speed until smooth. Add confectioners' sugar gradually and reserved ¼ teaspoon orange juice. Beat until creamy. Add additional orange juice, if necessary, until frosting is of desired spreading consistency. Frost top and sides of cake. Serve immediately or refrigerate until serving time. Refrigerate leftovers.

Makes 1 (13×9×2-inch) cake (12 to 16 Servings)

Choca-Cola Cake

CAKE

$1^3/_4$ cups granulated sugar

$^3/_4$ CRISCO® Stick or $^3/_4$ cup CRISCO® all-vegetable shortening

2 eggs

2 tablespoons unsweetened cocoa powder

1 tablespoon vanilla

$^1/_4$ teaspoon salt

$^1/_2$ cup buttermilk or sour milk*

1 teaspoon baking soda

$2^1/_2$ cups all-purpose flour

1 cup cola soft drink (not sugar-free)

FROSTING

1 box (1 pound) confectioners' sugar ($3^1/_2$ to 4 cups)

6 tablespoons or more cola soft drink (not sugar-free)

$^1/_4$ cup unsweetened cocoa powder

$^1/_4$ CRISCO® Stick or $^1/_4$ cup CRISCO® all-vegetable shortening

1 cup chopped pecans, divided

*To sour milk: Combine $1^1/_2$ teaspoons white vinegar plus enough milk to equal $^1/_2$ cup. Stir. Wait 5 minutes before using.

1. Heat oven to 350°F. Line bottom of 13×9×2-inch baking pan with waxed paper. Place wire rack on countertop for cooling cookies.

2. For cake, combine granulated sugar and $^3/_4$ cup shortening in large bowl. Beat at medium speed of electric mixer 1 minute. Add eggs. Beat until blended. Add 2 tablespoons cocoa, vanilla and salt. Beat until blended.

3. Combine buttermilk and baking soda in small bowl. Add to creamed mixture. Beat until blended. Reduce speed to low. Add flour alternately with 1 cup cola, beginning and ending with flour, beating at low speed after each addition until well blended. Pour into prepared pan.

4. Bake at 350°F for 30 to 35 minutes or until cake begins to pull away from sides of pan. *Do not overbake.* Cool 10 minutes before removing from pan. Invert cake onto wire rack. Remove waxed paper. Cool completely. Place cake on serving tray.

5. For frosting, combine confectioners' sugar, 6 tablespoons cola, 1/4 cup cocoa and 1/4 cup shortening in medium bowl. Beat at low, then medium speed until blended, adding more cola, if necessary, until frosting is of desired spreading consistency. Stir in 1/2 cup nuts. Frost top and sides of cake. Sprinkle remaining nuts over top of cake. Let stand at least 1 hour before serving.   *Makes 1 (13×9×2-inch) cake (12 to 16 servings)*

Note: Flavor of cake improves if made several hours or a day before serving.

Choca-Cola Cake

Carrot Cake

CAKE

$1\frac{1}{4}$ pounds carrots, peeled and cut lengthwise into 2-inch pieces (about 8 to 10 medium carrots)

2 cups granulated sugar

$1\frac{1}{2}$ CRISCO® Sticks or $1\frac{1}{2}$ cups CRISCO® all-vegetable shortening plus additional for greasing

4 eggs

$\frac{1}{2}$ cup water

2 cups all-purpose flour

1 tablespoon ground cinnamon

2 teaspoons baking soda

1 teaspoon salt

FROSTING

1 package (8 ounces) cream cheese, softened

$\frac{1}{2}$ Butter Flavor CRISCO® Stick or $\frac{1}{2}$ cup Butter Flavor CRISCO® all-vegetable shortening

1 box (1 pound) confectioners' sugar ($3\frac{1}{2}$ to 4 cups)

1 teaspoon vanilla

$\frac{1}{4}$ teaspoon salt

1. Heat oven to 350°F. Grease 13×9×2-inch insulated baking pan. Flour lightly. Place wire rack on countertop for cooling cake.

2. For cake, place carrots in food processor. Process until very fine and moist. Grate carrots very finely if food processor in unavailable. Measure 3 cups carrots.

3. Combine granulated sugar and $1\frac{1}{2}$ cups shortening in large bowl. Beat at medium speed of electric mixer until creamy. Beat in eggs until blended. Beat in water at low speed until blended.

58

4. Combine flour, cinnamon, baking soda and 1 teaspoon salt in medium bowl. Add to creamed mixture. Beat at low speed until blended. Beat 2 minutes at medium speed. Add carrots. Beat until well blended. Pour into prepared pan.

5. Bake at 350°F for 40 to 55 minutes or until toothpick inserted into center comes out clean. *Do not overbake.* Cool 10 minutes before removing from pan. Invert cake onto wire rack. Cool completely. Place cake on serving tray.

6. For frosting, combine cream cheese and $\frac{1}{2}$ cup shortening in large bowl. Beat at medium speed until blended. Reduce speed to low. Add confectioners' sugar, vanilla and $\frac{1}{4}$ teaspoon salt. Beat until blended. Beat at medium speed until frosting is of desired spreading consistency. Frost top and sides of cake. Garnish as desired.   *Makes 12 to 16 servings*

Carrot Cake

A Little Country Pumpkin Cake

CAKE

   2 cups boiling water

   $1/2$ cup raisins

   2 cups granulated sugar

   1 CRISCO® Stick or 1 cup CRISCO® all-vegetable shortening,
      melted plus additional for greasing

   1 can (16 ounces) solid-pack pumpkin (not pumpkin pie filling)

   4 eggs

   2 cups all-purpose flour

   1 tablespoon ground cinnamon

   2 teaspoons baking powder

   1 teaspoon baking soda

   1 teaspoon ground ginger

   $3/4$ teaspoon salt

   $1/4$ teaspoon ground cloves

FROSTING

   $1/4$ Butter Flavor CRISCO® Stick or $1/4$ cup Butter Flavor
      CRISCO® all-vegetable shortening

   2 cups confectioners' sugar

   3 tablespoons milk

   1 teaspoon vanilla

   Chopped nuts

1. Heat oven to 350°F. Grease 10-inch round cake pan. Flour lightly. Place wire rack on countertop for cooling cake.

2. For cake, pour boiling water over raisins in colander. Drain. Press lightly to remove excess water.

3. Combine granulated sugar, 1 cup melted shortening, pumpkin and eggs in large bowl. Beat at medium-high speed of electric mixer 5 minutes. Combine flour, cinnamon, baking powder, baking soda, ginger, salt and cloves in medium bowl. Add to pumpkin mixture, 1 cup at a time, beating at low speed after each addition until blended. Stir in raisins with spoon. Pour into prepared pan.

4. Bake at 350°F for 55 to 60 minutes or until toothpick inserted into center comes out clean. *Do not overbake.* Remove cake to rack to cool. Cool 10 to 15 minutes before removing from pan. Place cake, top side up, on wire rack. Cool completely. Place cake on serving plate.

5. For frosting, melt ¼ cup shortening in small saucepan on low heat. Transfer to medium bowl. Add confectioners' sugar. Beat at low, then high speed until blended. Add milk and vanilla. Beat at high speed until smooth and frosting is of desired spreading consistency. Frost top and side of cake. Press nuts into side of cake and around outside top edge.

Makes 1 (10-inch) round cake (10 to 12 servings)

A Little Country Pumpkin Cake

Gingerbread Cake with Lemon Sauce

CAKE

$^{1}/_{4}$ Butter Flavor CRISCO® Stick or $^{1}/_{4}$ cup Butter Flavor
   CRISCO® all-vegetable shortening

$^{1}/_{4}$ cup firmly packed light brown sugar

$^{1}/_{4}$ cup granulated sugar

 1 egg, beaten

$^{1}/_{2}$ cup buttermilk

$^{1}/_{4}$ cup light molasses

 1 cup all-purpose flour

 2 teaspoons ground ginger

 1 teaspoon ground cinnamon

$^{1}/_{2}$ teaspoon baking soda

$^{1}/_{4}$ teaspoon ground cloves

$^{1}/_{4}$ teaspoon freshly grated nutmeg

$^{1}/_{4}$ teaspoon salt

LEMON SAUCE

$^{1}/_{2}$ cup granulated sugar

$^{1}/_{4}$ cup unsalted butter

 3 tablespoons fresh lemon juice

 1 teaspoon vanilla

1. Heat oven to 375°F. Lightly spray 8-inch square or round cake pan
with CRISCO® No-Stick Cooking Spray; set aside. Place wire rack on
countertop for cooling cake.

2. For cake, combine $^{1}/_{4}$ cup shortening, brown sugar and $^{1}/_{4}$ cup
granulated sugar in large bowl. Beat at medium speed of electric mixer
until well blended. Beat in egg, buttermilk and molasses until well blended.

3. Combine flour, ginger, cinnamon, baking soda, cloves, nutmeg and salt in medium bowl. Add to creamed mixture; mix well. Pour batter into prepared pan.

4. Bake at 375°F for 20 to 25 minutes or until toothpick inserted into center comes out clean. Cool in pan 15 minutes. Turn out onto wire rack.

5. For Lemon Sauce, combine all ingredients in small saucepan. Bring to a boil over medium-high heat, stirring constantly. Reduce heat to low and simmer 5 minutes or until sauce is slightly thickened. Serve sauce over each slice of cake.   *Makes 6 to 8 servings*

Gingerbread Cake with Lemon Sauce

Traditional Cookies

Turn an ordinary day into something special—with some fresh-from-the-oven cookies and a tall, ice-cold glass of milk!

Black Forest Oatmeal Fancies

1 Butter Flavor CRISCO® Stick or 1 cup Butter Flavor
   CRISCO® all-vegetable shortening

1 cup firmly packed light brown sugar

1 cup granulated sugar

2 eggs

2 teaspoons vanilla

1 2/3 cups all-purpose flour

1 teaspoon baking soda

1 teaspoon salt

1/2 teaspoon baking powder

3 cups quick oats (not instant or old-fashioned), uncooked

1 baking bar (6 ounces) white chocolate, coarsely chopped

6 squares (1 ounce each) semisweet chocolate, coarsely chopped

1/2 cup coarsely chopped red candied cherries

1/2 cup sliced almonds

1. Heat oven to 375°F. Place foil on countertop for cooling cookies. Combine 1 cup shortening, brown sugar, granulated sugar, eggs and vanilla in large bowl. Beat at medium speed of electric mixer until well blended.

2. Combine flour, baking soda, salt and baking powder. Mix into shortening mixture at low speed until well blended. Stir in, one at a time, oats, white chocolate, semisweet chocolate, cherries and nuts with spoon.

3. Drop rounded tablespoonfuls of dough 2 inches apart onto ungreased baking sheets.

4. Bake at 375°F for 9 to 11 minutes or until set. *Do not overbake.* Cool 2 minutes on baking sheets. Remove cookies to foil to cool completely.

Makes about 3 dozen cookies

Irresistible Peanut Butter Cookies

1¼ cups firmly packed light brown sugar

¾ cup JIF® Creamy Peanut Butter

½ Butter Flavor CRISCO® Stick or ½ cup Butter Flavor
    CRISCO® all-vegetable shortening

3 tablespoons milk

1 tablespoon vanilla

1 egg

1¾ cups all-purpose flour

¾ teaspoon baking soda

¾ teaspoon salt

1. Heat oven to 375°F. Place sheets of foil on countertop for cooling cookies.

2. Combine brown sugar, peanut butter, ½ cup shortening, milk and vanilla in large bowl. Beat at medium speed of electric mixer until well blended. Add egg. Beat just until blended.

3. Combine flour, baking soda and salt. Add to creamed mixture at low speed. Mix just until blended.

4. Drop by rounded measuring tablespoonfuls of dough 2 inches apart onto ungreased baking sheet. Flatten slightly in crisscross pattern with tines of fork.

5. Bake one baking sheet at a time at 375°F for 7 to 8 minutes, or until set and just beginning to brown. *Do not overbake.* Cool 2 minutes on baking sheet. Remove cookies to foil to cool completely.

Makes about 3 dozen cookies

Irresistible Peanut Butter Cookies

Lollipop Sugar Cookies

1¼ cups granulated sugar

1 Butter Flavor CRISCO® Stick or 1 cup Butter Flavor
    CRISCO® all-vegetable shortening

2 eggs

¼ cup light corn syrup or regular pancake syrup

1 tablespoon vanilla

3 cups all-purpose flour

¾ teaspoon baking powder

½ teaspoon *each* baking soda and salt

36 flat ice cream sticks

    Any of the following: miniature baking chips, raisins, red hots,
    nonpareils, colored sugar or nuts

1. Combine sugar and 1 cup shortening in large bowl. Beat at medium speed of electric mixer until well blended. Add eggs, syrup and vanilla; beat until well blended and fluffy.

2. Combine flour, baking powder, baking soda and salt. Add gradually to creamed mixture at low speed until well blended. Wrap dough in plastic wrap. Refrigerate at least 1 hour.

3. Heat oven to 375°F. Place foil on countertop for cooling cookies.

4. Shape dough into 1½-inch balls. Push ice cream stick into center of each ball. Place balls 3 inches apart on ungreased baking sheet. Flatten balls to ½-inch thickness with bottom of greased and floured glass. Decorate as desired; press decorations gently into dough.

5. Bake at 375°F for 8 to 10 minutes. *Do not overbake.* Cool on baking sheet 2 minutes. Remove cookies to foil to cool completely.

Makes about 3 dozen cookies

Lollipop Sugar Cookies

Peanut Butter Kisses

1 1/4 cups firmly packed light brown sugar

3/4 cup JIF® Creamy Peanut Butter

1/2 CRISCO® Stick or 1/2 cup CRISCO® all-vegetable shortening

3 tablespoons milk

1 tablespoon vanilla

1 egg

1 3/4 cups all-purpose flour

3/4 teaspoon baking soda

3/4 teaspoon salt

Granulated sugar

48 chocolate kisses, unwrapped

1. Heat oven to 375°F. Place sheets of foil on countertop for cooling cookies.

2. Combine brown sugar, peanut butter, 1/2 cup shortening, milk and vanilla in large bowl. Beat at medium speed of electric mixer until well blended. Add egg. Beat just until blended.

3. Combine flour, baking soda and salt. Add to shortening mixture; beat at low speed just until blended.

4. Form dough into 1-inch balls. Roll in granulated sugar. Place 2 inches apart on ungreased baking sheets.

5. Bake one baking sheet at a time at 375°F for 6 minutes. Press chocolate kiss into center of each cookie. Return to oven. Bake 3 minutes. *Do not overbake.* Cool 2 minutes on baking sheets. Remove cookies to foil to cool completely.   *Makes about 3 dozen cookies*

Peanut Butter Kisses

Choco-Scutterbotch

$^2/_3$ Butter Flavor CRISCO® Stick or $^2/_3$ cup Butter Flavor
     CRISCO® all-vegetable shortening

$^1/_2$ cup firmly packed light brown sugar

 2 eggs

 1 package (18$^1/_4$ ounces) deluxe yellow cake mix

 1 cup toasted rice cereal

$^1/_2$ cup butterscotch chips

$^1/_2$ cup milk chocolate chunks

$^1/_2$ cup semisweet chocolate chips

$^1/_2$ cup coarsely chopped walnuts or pecans

1. Heat oven to 375°F. Place sheets of foil on countertop for cooling cookies.

2. Combine $^2/_3$ cup shortening and brown sugar in large bowl. Beat at medium speed of electric mixer until well blended. Beat in eggs.

3. Add cake mix gradually at low speed. Mix until well blended. Stir in cereal, butterscotch chips, chocolate chunks, chocolate chips and nuts. Stir until well blended.

4. Shape dough into 1$^1/_4$-inch balls. Place 2 inches apart on ungreased baking sheet. Flatten slightly. Shape sides to form circle, if necessary.

5. Bake at 375°F for 7 to 9 minutes or until lightly browned around edges. *Do not overbake.* Cool 2 minutes on baking sheet. Remove cookies to foil to cool completely.   *Makes 3 dozen cookies*

Choco-Scutterbotch

Cut-Out Sugar Cookies

1 1/4 cups granulated sugar

    1 Butter Flavor CRISCO® Stick or 1 cup Butter Flavor
        CRISCO® all-vegetable shortening

    2 eggs

1/4 cup light corn syrup or regular pancake syrup

    1 tablespoon vanilla

    3 cups plus 4 tablespoons all-purpose flour, divided

3/4 teaspoon baking powder

1/2 teaspoon baking soda

1/2 teaspoon salt

    Granulated sugar or colored sugar crystals

1. Combine sugar and 1 cup shortening in large bowl. Beat at medium speed of electric mixer until well blended. Add eggs, corn syrup and vanilla. Beat until well blended and fluffy.

2. Combine 3 cups flour, baking powder, baking soda and salt. Add gradually to shortening mixture at low speed. Mix until well blended.

3. Divide dough into 4 quarters. Wrap each quarter of dough with plastic wrap. Refrigerate at least 1 hour. Keep refrigerated until ready to use.

4. Heat oven to 375°F. Place sheets of foil on countertop for cooling cookies.

5. Spread 1 tablespoon flour on large sheet of waxed paper. Place one quarter of dough on floured paper. Flatten slightly with hands. Turn dough over and cover with another large sheet of waxed paper. Roll dough to 1/4-inch thickness. Remove top sheet of waxed paper. Cut out with floured cutters. Place 2 inches apart on ungreased baking sheets. Repeat with remaining dough.

6. Sprinkle cut-outs with granulated sugar or colored sugar crystals, or leave plain to frost or decorate when cooled.

7. Bake one baking sheet at a time at 375°F for 5 to 9 minutes, depending on size of cookies (bake smaller, thinner cookies closer to 5 minutes; larger cookies closer to 9 minutes). *Do not overbake.* Cool 2 minutes on baking sheets. Remove cookies to foil to cool completely, then frost and decorate, if desired.   *Makes about 3 to 4 dozen cookies*

Cut-Out Sugar Cookies

Chocolate Peanut Butter Cup Cookies

1 cup semisweet chocolate chips
2 squares (1 ounce each) unsweetened baking chocolate
1 cup granulated sugar
1/2 Butter Flavor CRISCO® Stick or 1/2 cup Butter Flavor CRISCO® all-vegetable shortening
2 eggs
1 teaspoon salt
1 teaspoon vanilla
1 1/2 cups plus 2 tablespoons all-purpose flour
1/2 teaspoon baking soda
3/4 cup finely chopped peanuts
36 miniature peanut butter cups, unwrapped
1 cup peanut butter chips

1. Heat oven to 350°F. Place sheets of foil on countertop for cooling cookies.

2. Combine chocolate chips and chocolate squares in microwave-safe measuring cup or bowl. Microwave at 50% power (MEDIUM). Stir after 2 minutes. Repeat until smooth (or melt on rangetop in small saucepan over very low heat). Cool slightly.

3. Combine sugar and 1/2 cup shortening in large bowl. Beat at medium speed of electric mixer until blended and crumbly. Beat in eggs, one at a time, then salt and vanilla. Reduce speed to low. Add chocolate slowly. Mix until well blended. Stir in flour and baking soda with spoon until well blended. Shape dough into 1 1/4-inch balls. Roll in nuts. Place 2 inches apart on ungreased baking sheet.

4. Bake at 350°F for 8 to 10 minutes or until set. *Do not overbake.* Press peanut butter cup into center of each cookie immediately. Cool 2 minutes on baking sheet. Remove cookies to foil to cool completely.

5. Place peanut butter chips in heavy resealable sandwich bag. Seal. Microwave at 50% power (MEDIUM). Knead bag after 1 minute. Repeat until smooth (or melt by placing bag in hot water). Cut tiny tip off corner of bag. Squeeze out and drizzle over cookies. *Makes 3 dozen cookies*

Chocolate Peanut Butter Cup Cookies

Ali's Oatmeal Cookies

1 Butter Flavor CRISCO® Stick or 1 cup Butter Flavor
   CRISCO® all-vegetable shortening
1 cup *each* granulated sugar and firmly packed light brown sugar
2 eggs
1 teaspoon vanilla
1 1/2 cups plus 1 tablespoon all-purpose flour, divided
1 teaspoon baking soda
3/4 teaspoon salt
2 1/2 cups quick or old-fashioned oats (not instant), uncooked
1 cup finely chopped hazelnuts
1 cup finely diced dried apricots
1 cup chopped white chocolate chips

1. Heat oven to 350°F. Place sheets of foil on countertop for cooling cookies.

2. Mix 1 cup shortening, granulated sugar, brown sugar, eggs and vanilla in large bowl. Beat at medium speed of electric mixer until well blended.

3. Combine 1 1/2 cups flour, baking soda and salt. Add gradually to creamed mixture at low speed. Beat until well blended. Stir in oats and nuts with spoon.

4. Toss apricots with remaining 1 tablespoon flour. Stir into dough. Stir in white chocolate chips. Shape dough into 1 1/2-inch balls. Flatten slightly. Place 2 inches apart on ungreased baking sheet.

5. Bake at 350°F for 11 to 13 minutes or until just beginning to brown around edges and slightly moist in center. *Do not overbake.* Cool 2 minutes on baking sheet. Remove cookies to foil to cool completely.

Makes about 3 dozen cookies

Ali's Oatmeal Cookies

Peanut Butter and Jelly Sandwich Surprises

1 1/2 cups all-purpose flour

1/2 cup plus 1 tablespoon granulated sugar

1/2 teaspoon baking soda

1/4 teaspoon salt

1/2 cup JIF® Creamy Peanut Butter

1/3 Butter Flavor CRISCO® Stick or 1/3 cup Butter Flavor
    CRISCO® all-vegetable shortening

3 tablespoons milk

1 egg yolk

1 teaspoon vanilla

SMUCKER'S® Concord Grape Jelly

Granulated sugar

1. Combine flour, 1/2 cup plus 1 tablespoon sugar, baking soda and salt
in large bowl. Cut in peanut butter and 1/3 cup shortening using pastry
blender or 2 knives until mixture resembles coarse meal.

2. Combine milk, egg yolk and vanilla in small bowl. Beat with fork until
blended. Add to flour mixture. Beat at low speed of electric mixer until
well blended. Divide dough in half. Wrap with plastic wrap. Refrigerate at
least 1 hour.

3. Heat oven to 350°F. Place sheets of foil on countertop for cooling
cookies.

4. Roll each half of dough between sheets of plastic wrap to 1/8-inch
thickness. Cut with 2 1/2-inch heart-shaped cookie cutter. Place half the
cut-outs 1 inch apart on ungreased baking sheets. Place about 1/2 teaspoon

jelly in center of each. Top with remaining cut-outs. Press edges with fork. Prick top several times with toothpick. Sprinkle lightly with sugar.

5. Bake at 350°F for 10 to 11 minutes or until golden brown. *Do not overbake.* Sprinkle again with sugar. Cool on baking sheet 5 minutes. Remove cookies to foil to cool completely.

Makes about 2 dozen cookies

Peanut Butter and Jelly Sandwich Surprises

Snickerdoodles

2 cups granulated sugar, divided
1 Butter Flavor CRISCO® Stick or 1 cup Butter Flavor
    CRISCO® all-vegetable shortening
2 eggs
2 tablespoons milk
1 teaspoon vanilla
2³/₄ cups all-purpose flour
2 teaspoons cream of tartar
1 teaspoon baking soda
³/₄ teaspoon salt
2 teaspoons ground cinnamon

1. Heat oven to 400°F. Place sheets of foil on countertop for cooling cookies.

2. Combine 1¹/₂ cups sugar, 1 cup shortening, eggs, milk and vanilla in large bowl. Beat at medium speed of electric mixer until well blended.

3. Combine flour, cream of tartar, baking soda and salt. Add gradually to creamed mixture at low speed. Mix just until blended. Shape dough into 1-inch balls.

4. Combine remaining ¹/₂ cup sugar and cinnamon in small bowl. Roll balls of dough in mixture. Place 2 inches apart on ungreased baking sheet.

5. Bake at 400°F for 7 to 8 minutes. *Do not overbake.* Cool 2 minutes on baking sheet. Remove cookies to foil to cool completely.

Makes 6 dozen cookies

Hint: Cinnamon-sugar mixture can be put in resealable plastic bag. Put 2 to 3 dough balls at a time in bag. Seal. Shake to sugar-coat dough.

Maple Walnut Cookies

1 1/4 cups firmly packed light brown sugar

3/4 Butter Flavor CRISCO® Stick or 3/4 cup Butter Flavor
CRISCO® all-vegetable shortening

2 tablespoons maple syrup

1 teaspoon vanilla

1 teaspoon maple extract

1 egg

1 3/4 cups all-purpose flour

1 teaspoon salt

3/4 teaspoon baking soda

1/2 teaspoon ground cinnamon

1 1/2 cups chopped walnuts

30 to 40 walnut halves

1. Heat oven to 375°F. Place sheets of foil on countertop for cooling cookies.

2. Place brown sugar, 3/4 cup shortening, maple syrup, vanilla and maple extract in large bowl. Beat at medium speed of electric mixer until well blended. Add egg; beat well.

3. Combine flour, salt, baking soda and cinnamon. Add to shortening mixture; beat at low speed just until blended. Stir in chopped walnuts.

4. Drop by rounded measuring tablespoonfuls of dough 3 inches apart onto ungreased baking sheets. Press walnut half into center of each cookie.

5. Bake one baking sheet at a time at 375°F for 8 to 10 minutes for chewy cookies, or 11 to 13 minutes for crisp cookies. *Do not overbake.* Cool 2 minutes on baking sheets. Remove cookies to foil to cool completely.   *Makes about 3 dozen cookies*

Double Chocolate Cherry Cookies

COOKIES

- 1$^1/_2$ cups firmly packed light brown sugar
- $^2/_3$ CRISCO® Stick or $^2/_3$ cup CRISCO® all-vegetable shortening
- 1 tablespoon water
- 1 teaspoon vanilla
- 2 eggs
- 1$^1/_2$ cups all-purpose flour
- $^1/_3$ cup unsweetened cocoa powder
- $^1/_2$ teaspoon salt
- $^1/_4$ teaspoon baking soda
- 30 to 40 maraschino cherries

ICING

- $^1/_2$ cup semisweet chocolate chips or white chocolate chips
- $^1/_2$ teaspoon CRISCO® Stick or CRISCO® all-vegetable shortening

1. Heat oven to 375°F. Place sheets of foil on countertop for cooling cookies.

2. For cookies, place brown sugar, $^2/_3$ cup shortening, water and vanilla in large bowl. Beat at medium speed of electric mixer until well blended. Add eggs; beat well.

3. Combine flour, cocoa, salt and baking soda. Add to shortening mixture; beat at low speed just until blended.

4. Shape rounded measuring tablespoonfuls of dough around each maraschino cherry, covering cherry completely. Place cookies 2 inches apart on ungreased baking sheet.

5. Bake one baking sheet at a time at 375°F for 7 to 9 minutes or until cookies are set. *Do not overbake.* Cool 2 minutes on baking sheet. Remove cookies to foil to cool completely.

6. For icing, place chocolate chips and ½ teaspoon shortening in heavy resealable sandwich bag; seal bag. Microwave at 50% power (MEDIUM) for 1 minute. Knead bag. If necessary, microwave at 50% power another 30 seconds at a time until mixture is smooth when bag is kneaded. Cut small tip off corner of bag; drizzle chocolate over cookies.

Makes about 3 dozen cookies

Double Chocolate Cherry Cookies

Anna's Icing Oatmeal Sandwich Cookies

COOKIES

$^{3}/_{4}$ Butter Flavor CRISCO® Stick or $^{3}/_{4}$ cup Butter Flavor
    CRISCO® all-vegetable shortening plus additional for
    greasing

$1^{1}/_{4}$ cups firmly packed light brown sugar

1 egg

$^{1}/_{3}$ cup milk

$1^{1}/_{2}$ teaspoons vanilla

3 cups quick oats (not instant or old-fashioned), uncooked

1 cup all-purpose flour

$^{1}/_{2}$ teaspoon baking soda

$^{1}/_{2}$ teaspoon salt

FROSTING

2 cups confectioners' sugar

$^{1}/_{4}$ Butter Flavor CRISCO® Stick or $^{1}/_{4}$ cup Butter Flavor
    CRISCO® all-vegetable shortening

$^{1}/_{2}$ teaspoon vanilla

Milk

1. Heat oven to 350°F. Grease baking sheets with shortening. Place sheets of foil on countertop for cooling cookies.

2. For cookies, combine $^{3}/_{4}$ cup shortening, brown sugar, egg, milk and $1^{1}/_{2}$ teaspoons vanilla in large bowl. Beat at medium speed of electric mixer until well blended.

3. Combine oats, flour, baking soda and salt. Mix into creamed mixture at low speed just until blended.

4. Drop rounded measuring tablespoonfuls of dough 2 inches apart onto prepared baking sheets.

5. Bake one sheet at a time at 375°F for 10 to 12 minutes or until lightly browned. *Do not overbake.* Cool 2 minutes on baking sheet. Remove cookies to foil to cool completely.

6. For frosting, combine confectioners' sugar, $^1/_4$ cup shortening and $^1/_2$ teaspoon vanilla in medium bowl. Beat at low speed, adding enough milk for good spreading consistency. Spread on bottoms of half the cookies. Top with remaining cookies.   *Makes about 16 sandwich cookies*

Anna's Icing Oatmeal Sandwich Cookies

Sour Cream Chocolate Chip Cookies

1 Butter Flavor CRISCO® Stick or 1 cup Butter Flavor
   CRISCO® all-vegetable shortening plus additional for
   greasing
1 cup firmly packed light brown sugar
1/2 cup granulated sugar
1 egg
1/2 cup dairy sour cream
1/4 cup honey, warmed
2 teaspoons vanilla
2 1/2 cups all-purpose flour
1 1/2 teaspoons baking powder
1/2 teaspoon salt
2 cups semisweet or milk chocolate chips
1 cup coarsely chopped walnuts

1. Heat oven to 375°F. Grease baking sheet. Place sheets of foil on
countertop for cooling cookies.

2. Combine 1 cup shortening, brown sugar and granulated sugar in large
bowl. Beat at medium speed of electric mixer until well blended. Beat in
egg, sour cream, honey and vanilla. Beat just until blended.

3. Combine flour, baking powder and salt. Mix into creamed mixture at
low speed just until blended. Stir in chocolate chips and nuts.

4. Drop slightly rounded measuring tablespoonfuls of dough 2 inches
apart onto prepared baking sheet.

5. Bake at 375°F 10 to 12 minutes or until set. *Do not overbake.* Cool
2 minutes on baking sheet. Remove to foil to cool completely.

Makes about 5 dozen cookies

Sour Cream Chocolate Chip Cookies

Lemon Pecan Cookies

1 Butter Flavor CRISCO® Stick or 1 cup Butter Flavor
    CRISCO® all-vegetable shortening
1 1/2 cups granulated sugar
2 eggs
3 tablespoons fresh lemon juice
3 cups all-purpose flour
2 teaspoons baking powder
1/4 teaspoon salt
1 cup chopped pecans

1. Heat oven to 350°F. Place wire rack on countertop for cooling cookies.

2. Combine 1 cup shortening and sugar in large bowl. Beat at medium speed of electric mixer until well blended. Beat in eggs and lemon juice until well blended.

3. Combine flour, baking powder and salt in medium bowl. Add to creamed mixture; mix well. Stir in pecans. Spray baking sheets lightly with CRISCO® No-Stick Cooking Spray. Drop dough by teaspoonfuls about 2 inches apart onto prepared baking sheets. Bake at 350°F for 10 for 12 minutes or until lightly browned. Cool on baking sheets 4 minutes; transfer to wire rack to cool completely.   *Makes about 6 dozen cookies*

Lemon Pecan Cookies

Dandy Candy Oatmeal Cookies

1 jar (12 ounces) JIF® Creamy Peanut Butter

1 cup granulated sugar

1 cup firmly packed light brown sugar

$^1/_2$ Butter Flavor CRISCO® Stick or $^1/_2$ cup Butter Flavor
CRISCO® all-vegetable shortening plus additional for
greasing

3 eggs

$^3/_4$ teaspoon vanilla

$^3/_4$ teaspoon maple (or maple-blend) syrup

2 teaspoons baking soda

$4^1/_2$ cups quick oats (not instant or old-fashioned), uncooked,
divided

1 package (8 ounces) candy-coated chocolate pieces

1. Heat oven to 350°F. Grease baking sheet with shortening. Place sheets of foil on countertop for cooling cookies.

2. Combine peanut butter, granulated sugar, brown sugar and $^1/_2$ cup shortening in large bowl. Beat at medium speed of electric mixer until well blended and fluffy. Add eggs, vanilla and maple syrup. Beat at high speed 3 to 4 minutes. Add baking soda and $2^1/_4$ cups oats; stir. Stir in candy. Stir in remaining $2^1/_4$ cups oats. Shape dough into $1^1/_2$-inch balls. Flatten slightly. Place 2 inches apart on prepared baking sheet.

3. Bake at 350°F for 9 to 10 minutes for chewy cookies or 11 to 12 minutes for crispy cookies. Cool 2 minutes. Remove cookies to foil to cool completely.   *Makes 3$^1/_2$ dozen cookies*

Dandy Candy Oatmeal Cookies

Oatmeal Coconut Chocolate Chip Cookies

COOKIES

    1 Butter Flavor CRISCO® Stick or 1 cup Butter Flavor CRISCO® all-vegetable shortening plus additional for greasing

    1 cup granulated sugar

    $1/2$ cup firmly packed light brown sugar

    2 eggs

    2 teaspoons vanilla

    2 cups all-purpose flour

    1 teaspoon salt

    1 teaspoon baking soda

    $2/3$ cup quick oats (not instant or old-fashioned), uncooked

    $1/2$ cup flake coconut

    1 cup semisweet chocolate chips

CHOCOLATE COATING

    1 cup semisweet chocolate chips

    2 teaspoons Butter Flavor CRISCO® Stick or 2 teaspoons Butter Flavor CRISCO® all-vegetable shortening

1. Heat oven to 375°F. Grease baking sheet with shortening. Place sheets of foil on countertop for cooling cookies.

2. For cookies, combine 1 cup shortening, granulated sugar, brown sugar, eggs and vanilla in large bowl. Beat at medium speed of electric mixer until well blended.

3. Combine flour, salt and baking soda. Add gradually to creamed mixture at low speed. Beat until well blended. Stir in oats, coconut and 1 cup

chocolate chips with spoon. Drop by teaspoonfuls 2 inches apart onto prepared baking sheet.

4. Bake at 375°F for 10 to 12 minutes or until light brown. *Do not overbake.* Cool 2 minutes on baking sheet. Remove cookies to foil to cool completely.

5. For chocolate coating, place 1 cup chocolate chips and 2 teaspoons shortening in small microwave-safe measuring cup or bowl. Microwave at 50% (MEDIUM). Stir after 1 minute. Repeat until melted and smooth.

6. Spread thin coating of melted chocolate on back of each cookie. Place upside down on waxed paper to allow coating to harden.

Makes about 6 dozen cookies

Oatmeal Coconut Chocolate Chip Cookies

Bar Cookie Classics

No one can resist deliciously moist
bar cookies. The aroma of these
easy-to-bake treats will bring family
and neighbors running into the kitchen!

Chocolate Chip Cookie Bars

1 1/4 cups firmly packed light brown sugar

3/4 Butter Flavor CRISCO® Stick or 3/4 cup Butter Flavor
    CRISCO® all-vegetable shortening plus additional for
    greasing

2 tablespoons milk

1 tablespoon vanilla

1 egg

1 3/4 cups all-purpose flour

1 teaspoon salt

3/4 teaspoon baking soda

1 cup (6 ounces) semisweet chocolate chips

1 cup coarsely chopped pecans* (optional)

*If pecans are omitted, add an additional 1/2 cup semisweet chocolate chips.

1. Heat oven to 350°F. Grease 13×9×2-inch baking pan. Place wire rack on countertop for cooling bars.

2. Combine brown sugar, 3/4 cup shortening, milk and vanilla in large bowl. Beat at medium speed of electric mixer until well blended. Add egg; beat well.

3. Combine flour, salt and baking soda. Add to creamed mixture; beat at low speed just until blended. Stir in chocolate chips and nuts, if desired.

4. Press dough evenly onto bottom of prepared pan.

5. Bake at 350°F for 20 to 25 minutes or until lightly browned and firm in the center. *Do not overbake.* Cool completely on wire rack. Cut into 2×1 1/2-inch bars. *Makes about 3 dozen bars*

Emily's Dream Bars

$^{1}/_{2}$ Butter Flavor CRISCO® Stick or $^{1}/_{2}$ cup Butter Flavor
  CRISCO® all-vegetable shortening plus additional for
  greasing
1 cup JIF® Crunchy Peanut Butter
$^{1}/_{2}$ cup firmly packed light brown sugar
$^{1}/_{2}$ cup light corn syrup
1 egg
1 teaspoon vanilla
1 cup all-purpose flour
$^{1}/_{2}$ teaspoon baking powder
$^{1}/_{4}$ cup milk
2 cups 100% natural oat, honey and raisin cereal
1 package (12 ounces) miniature semisweet chocolate chips
  (2 cups), divided
1 cup almond brickle chips
1 cup milk chocolate covered peanuts
1 package (2 ounces) nut topping ($^{1}/_{3}$ cup)

1. Heat oven to 350°F. Grease 13×9×2-inch baking pan with shortening. Place wire rack on countertop for cooling bars.

2. Combine $^{1}/_{2}$ cup shortening, peanut butter, brown sugar and corn syrup in large bowl. Beat at medium speed of electric mixer until creamy. Add egg and vanilla. Beat well.

3. Combine flour and baking powder. Add alternately with milk to creamed mixture at medium speed. Stir in cereal, 1 cup chocolate chips, almond brickle chips and chocolate covered nuts with spoon. Spread in prepared pan.

4. Bake at 350°F for 20 to 26 minutes or until golden brown and toothpick inserted into center comes out clean. *Do not overbake.* Sprinkle remaining 1 cup chocolate chips over top immediately after removing from oven. Remove pan to wire rack. Let stand about 3 to 5 minutes or until chips become shiny and soft. Spread over top. Sprinkle with nut topping. Cool completely. Cut into 2×1-inch bars.

Makes 4½ dozen bars

Emily's Dream Bars

Chocolate Chip Pecan Squares

$^{1}/_{2}$ Butter Flavor CRISCO® Stick or $^{1}/_{2}$ cup Butter Flavor
 CRISCO® all-vegetable shortening plus additional for
 greasing
$^{1}/_{2}$ cup firmly packed light brown sugar
 1 egg
 1 tablespoon milk
 1 teaspoon vanilla
$^{3}/_{4}$ cup all-purpose flour
 2 cups milk chocolate chips,* divided
$^{3}/_{4}$ cup chopped pecans
 Additional $^{1}/_{4}$ cup chopped pecans for garnish (optional)

*You can substitute semisweet chocolate chips for the milk chocolate chips.

1. Heat oven to 350°F. Grease 8×8×2-inch baking pan with shortening. Place wire rack on countertop for cooling squares.

2. Combine $^{1}/_{2}$ cup shortening, brown sugar, egg, milk and vanilla in large bowl. Beat at medium speed of electric mixer until well blended.

3. Mix in flour at low speed. Stir in 1 cup chocolate chips and $^{1}/_{2}$ cup nuts. Spread in prepared pan.

4. Bake at 350°F for 25 to 30 minutes or until lightly browned. Remove from oven. Sprinkle with remaining 1 cup chocolate chips. Wait 3 to 5 minutes until chips become shiny and soft. Spread evenly. Sprinkle additional $^{1}/_{4}$ cup nuts over top, if desired. Cool completely in pan on wire rack. Cut into 2×2-inch squares.   *Makes 16 squares*

Top to bottom: Chocolate Chip Pecan Squares and Streusel Peanut Butter Bars (page 108)

Apple Date Nut Blondies

2 medium Granny Smith or other firm, tart cooking apples,
peeled, cored and finely chopped

2½ cups all-purpose flour, divided

1 cup firmly packed light brown sugar

¾ Butter Flavor CRISCO® Stick or ¾ cup Butter Flavor
CRISCO® all-vegetable shortening plus additional for
greasing

2 eggs

2 tablespoons vanilla

2 teaspoons baking powder

½ teaspoon salt

½ cup finely chopped pecans

½ cup finely chopped dates

Confectioners' sugar

1. Heat oven to 350°F. Grease 15×10×1-inch jelly-roll pan with shortening. Place wire rack on countertop for cooling bars.

2. Toss apples with ¼ cup flour.

3. Combine brown sugar and ¾ cup shortening in large bowl. Beat at medium speed of electric mixer until blended. Beat in eggs and vanilla.

4. Combine remaining 2¼ cups flour, baking powder and salt. Add gradually to creamed mixture at low speed. Beat until well blended. Fold in apple mixture, nuts and dates. Spread in prepared pan.

5. Bake at 350°F for 25 to 30 minutes or until toothpick inserted in center comes out clean. *Do not overbake.* Remove pan to wire rack. Cool completely. Cut into 2½×1½-inch bars. Dust with confectioners' sugar just before serving.   *Makes about 3 dozen bars*

Chewy Macadamia Nut Blondies

3/4 Butter Flavor CRISCO® Stick or 3/4 cup Butter Flavor
    CRISCO® all-vegetable shortening
1 cup firmly packed light brown sugar
1 egg
1 teaspoon vanilla
1 teaspoon almond extract
1 cup all-purpose flour
1/2 teaspoon baking soda
1/8 teaspoon salt
6 ounces white chocolate chips
1 cup chopped macadamia nuts

1. Heat oven to 325°F. Place wire rack on countertop for cooling bars.

2. Combine 3/4 cup shortening and brown sugar in large bowl. Beat at medium speed of electric mixer until well blended. Beat in egg, vanilla and almond extract until well blended.

3. Combine flour, baking soda and salt in small bowl. Add to creamed mixture just until incorporated. *Do not overmix.* Fold in white chocolate chips and nuts just until blended.

4. Spray 9-inch square baking pan with CRISCO® No-Stick Cooking Spray. Pour batter into prepared pan. Bake at 325°F for 25 to 30 minutes or until toothpick inserted into center comes out almost dry and top is golden. *Do not overbake.*

5. Cool completely in pan on wire rack. Cut into bars.

Makes about 16 bars

Chippy Cheeseys

BASE
1 1/4 cups firmly packed light brown sugar
3/4 Butter Flavor CRISCO® stick or 3/4 cup Butter Flavor
    CRISCO® all-vegetable shortening plus additional for
    greasing
2 tablespoons milk
1 egg
1 tablespoon vanilla
2 cups all-purpose flour
1 teaspoon salt
3/4 teaspoon baking soda
1 cup (6 ounces) miniature semisweet chocolate chips
1 cup finely chopped walnuts

FILLING
2 packages (8 ounces each) cream cheese, softened
2 eggs
3/4 cup granulated sugar
1 teaspoon vanilla

1. Heat oven to 375°F. Grease 13×9-inch baking pan with shortening.
Place wire rack on countertop for cooling bars.

2. For base, combine brown sugar and 3/4 cup shortening in large bowl.
Beat at medium speed of electric mixer until creamy. Beat in milk, 1 egg
and 1 tablespoon vanilla.

3. Combine flour, salt and baking soda. Add gradually to creamed mixture
at low speed. Stir in chocolate chips and nuts with spoon. Spread half of
dough in prepared pan. Bake at 375°F for 8 minutes. *Do not overbake.*

4. For filling, combine cream cheese, 2 eggs, granulated sugar and 1 teaspoon vanilla in medium bowl. Beat at medium speed of electric mixer until smooth. Pour over hot crust.

5. Roll remaining half of dough between sheets of waxed paper into 13×9-inch rectangle. Remove top sheet of waxed paper. Flip dough over onto filling. Remove waxed paper.

6. Bake at 375°F for 40 minutes or until top is set and light golden brown. *Do not overbake.* Remove pan to wire rack to cool to room temperature. Cut into 2×1¾-inch bars. Refrigerate. *Makes about 30 bars*

Chippy Cheeseys

Cream Cheese Swirled Brownies

FILLING

- ⅓ Butter Flavor CRISCO® Stick or ⅓ cup Butter Flavor CRISCO® all-vegetable shortening plus additional for greasing
- 1 package (8 ounces) cream cheese, softened
- 1 teaspoon vanilla
- ½ cup granulated sugar
- 2 eggs
- 3 tablespoons all-purpose flour

BROWNIE

- ⅔ Butter Flavor CRISCO® Stick or ⅔ cup Butter Flavor CRISCO® all-vegetable shortening
- 4 squares unsweetened baking chocolate
- 2 cups granulated sugar
- 4 eggs
- 1 teaspoon vanilla
- 1¼ cups all-purpose flour
- 1 teaspoon baking powder
- 1 teaspoon salt

1. Heat oven to 350°F. Grease 13×9×2-inch baking pan with shortening. Place wire rack on countertop for cooling brownies.

2. For filling, combine ⅓ cup shortening, cream cheese and vanilla in small bowl. Beat at medium speed of electric mixer until well blended. Beat in ½ cup sugar. Add 2 eggs, 1 at a time; beat well after each addition. Beat in 3 tablespoons flour; set aside.

3. For brownie, melt ⅔ cup shortening and chocolate in large saucepan on low heat. Remove from heat. Stir 2 cups sugar into melted chocolate

mixture with spoon. Stir 1 egg at a time quickly into hot mixture until well blended. Stir in vanilla.

4. Combine 1¼ cups flour, baking powder and salt. Stir gradually into chocolate mixture.

5. Spread half the chocolate mixture in prepared pan. Drop cheese mixture over chocolate layer. Spread gently to cover. Drop remaining chocolate mixture over cream cheese layer. Spread gently to cover. Swirl 2 mixtures together using tip of knife.**

6. Bake at 350°F for 35 minutes. *Do not overbake.* Remove pan to wire rack to cool completely. Cut into 2×2-inch squares.

Makes about 2 dozen brownies

****A nice swirl design depends on how much you pull knife through batter. Do not overdo.*

Cream Cheese Swirled Brownies

Streusel Peanut Butter Bars

BASE

$^1/_2$ Butter Flavor CRISCO® Stick or $^1/_2$ cup Butter Flavor CRISCO®
all-vegetable shortening plus additional for greasing

$1^1/_2$ cups firmly packed light brown sugar

$^2/_3$ cup JIF® Creamy or Crunchy Peanut Butter

2 eggs

1 teaspoon vanilla

$1^1/_2$ cups all-purpose flour

$^1/_2$ teaspoon salt

$^1/_4$ cup milk

STREUSEL TOPPING

3 tablespoons Butter Flavor CRISCO® Stick or 3 tablespoons
Butter Flavor CRISCO® all-vegetable shortening

$^1/_3$ cup all-purpose flour

$^1/_3$ cup firmly packed light brown sugar

1 tablespoon JIF® Creamy or Crunchy Peanut Butter

$^1/_4$ cup finely chopped peanuts

1. Heat oven to 350°F. Grease 13×9×2-inch baking pan with shortening. Place wire rack on countertop for cooling bars.

2. For base, combine $^1/_2$ cup shortening, $1^1/_2$ cups brown sugar and $^2/_3$ cup peanut butter in large bowl. Beat at medium speed of electric mixer until well blended. Beat in eggs and vanilla.

3. Combine $1^1/_2$ cups flour and salt. Add alternately with milk to creamed mixture at low speed. Beat until well blended. Spread in prepared pan.

4. For topping, combine 3 tablespoons shortening, $^1/_3$ cup flour, $^1/_3$ cup brown sugar and 1 tablespoon peanut butter. Mix with spoon until well

blended and coarse crumbs form. Sprinkle over unbaked base. Sprinkle nuts over top.

5. Bake at 350°F for 30 to 33 minutes or until golden brown and center is set. *Do not overbake.* Cool completely in pan on wire rack. Cut into 2¼×1½-inch bars. *Makes 32 bars*

Butterscotch Brownies

2 eggs
2 cups firmly packed light brown sugar
½ Butter Flavor CRISCO® Stick or ½ cup Butter Flavor
    CRISCO® all-vegetable shortening, melted, plus additional
    for greasing
1 teaspoon vanilla
1½ cups all-purpose flour
2 teaspoons baking powder
½ teaspoon salt
1 cup finely chopped walnuts or pecans

1. Heat oven to 350°F. Grease 13×9×2-inch baking pan with shortening. Place wire rack on countertop for cooling brownies.

2. Beat eggs in large bowl at medium speed of electric mixer until light and foamy. Add brown sugar, ½ cup shortening and vanilla. Beat until creamy.

3. Combine flour, baking powder and salt. Add gradually to egg mixture at low speed until blended. Mix in nuts. (Dough will be stiff.) Spread in prepared pan.

4. Bake at 350°F for 25 to 30 minutes or until top is light brown and toothpick inserted into center comes out clean. Cool 10 to 15 minutes on wire rack. Cut into 2½×2-inch bars. *Makes 2 dozen bars*

Peanut Butter and Jelly Crispies

$^1/_2$ Butter Flavor CRISCO® Stick or $^1/_2$ cup Butter Flavor CRISCO®
all-vegetable shortening plus additional for greasing
$^1/_2$ cup JIF® Crunchy Peanut Butter
$^1/_2$ cup granulated sugar
$^1/_2$ cup firmly packed light brown sugar
1 egg
1$^1/_4$ cups all-purpose flour
$^1/_2$ teaspoon baking powder
$^1/_2$ teaspoon baking soda
$^1/_4$ teaspoon salt
2 cups crisp rice cereal
Honey roasted peanuts, finely chopped (optional)
SMUCKER'S® Jelly, any flavor

1. Heat oven to 375°F. Grease 13×9×2-inch baking pan with shortening. Place wire rack on countertop for cooling bars.

2. Combine $^1/_2$ cup shortening, peanut butter, granulated sugar and brown sugar in large bowl. Beat at medium speed of electric mixer until well blended. Beat in egg.

3. Combine flour, baking powder, baking soda and salt. Add gradually to creamed mixture at low speed. Beat until well blended. Add cereal. Mix just until blended. Press into prepared pan. Sprinkle with nuts, if desired.

4. Score dough into bars about 2$^1/_4$×2 inches. Press thumb in center of each bar. Fill indentation with $^1/_4$ to $^1/_2$ teaspoon jelly.

5. Bake at 375°F for 12 to 15 minutes or until golden brown. *Do not overbake.* Remove pan to wire rack. Cool 2 to 3 minutes. Cut into bars. Cool completely.   *Makes about 2 dozen bars*

Peanut Butter and Jelly Crispies

Chocolate Coconut Bars

COOKIE BASE

$^2/_3$ cup granulated sugar

$^1/_2$ Butter Flavor CRISCO® Stick or $^1/_2$ cup Butter Flavor
CRISCO® all-vegetable shortening plus additional for
greasing

$^1/_4$ cup unsweetened cocoa powder

1 egg

1 tablespoon water

1$^1/_4$ cups all-purpose flour

$^1/_4$ teaspoon salt

FILLING

1 can (14 ounces) sweetened condensed milk (not evaporated
milk)

3 tablespoons all-purpose flour

1 teaspoon vanilla

$^3/_4$ cup semisweet chocolate chips

$^2/_3$ cup chopped walnuts

$^1/_2$ cup flake coconut

1. Heat oven to 350°F. Grease 13×9×2-inch baking pan with
shortening. Place wire rack on countertop for cooling bars.

2. For cookie base, combine sugar, $^1/_2$ cup shortening, cocoa, egg and water
in large bowl. Beat at medium speed of electric mixer until well blended.

3. Combine 1$^1/_4$ cups flour and salt. Add gradually to creamed mixture at
low speed. Beat just until blended. Press into bottom of prepared pan.

4. Bake at 350°F for 10 minutes. *Do not overbake.*

5. For filling, combine condensed milk, 3 tablespoons flour and vanilla. Stir with spoon until well blended. Stir in chocolate chips, nuts and coconut. Spoon over partially baked cookie base. Spread carefully to cover.

6. Return to oven. Bake at 350°F for 20 minutes. *Do not overbake.* Remove pan to wire rack to cool completely. Cut into $1^1/_2 \times 1^1/_2$-inch bars.

Makes about 4 dozen bars

Chocolate Coconut Bars

Magic Apple Cookie Bars

1 cup quick oats (not instant or old-fashioned), uncooked

$^3/_4$ cup graham cracker crumbs

$^1/_4$ Butter Flavor CRISCO® Stick or $^1/_4$ cup Butter Flavor CRISCO® all-vegetable shortening plus additional for greasing

$1^1/_2$ cups very finely chopped peeled Granny Smith or other firm, tart cooking apples

$^1/_2$ cup butterscotch chips (optional)

$^1/_2$ cup flake coconut

$^1/_2$ cup finely chopped nuts

1 can (14 ounces) sweetened condensed milk (not evaporated milk)

1. Heat oven to 350°F. Grease 11×7×2-inch glass baking dish with shortening. Place wire rack on countertop for cooling bars.

2. Combine oats, graham cracker crumbs and $^1/_4$ cup shortening. Stir well. Press firmly on bottom of prepared dish. Top with apples, butterscotch chips, coconut and nuts. Pour condensed milk over top.

3. Bake at 350°F for 30 to 35 minutes or until lightly browned. *Do not overbake.* Loosen from sides of dish while still warm. Cool completely in pan on wire rack. Cut into 2×1$^1/_2$-inch bars. Serve immediately or refrigerate. *Makes 3 dozen bars*

Outlandish Oatmeal Bars

¾ Butter Flavor CRISCO® Stick or ¾ cup Butter Flavor CRISCO®
    all-vegetable shortening plus additional for greasing

¾ cup firmly packed light brown sugar

½ cup granulated sugar

1 egg

¼ cup SMUCKER'S® Apple Butter

2 tablespoons milk

1¼ cups all-purpose flour

½ teaspoon baking soda

½ teaspoon salt

2½ cups quick oats (not instant or old-fashioned), uncooked

1 cup SMUCKER'S® Raspberry Preserves, stirred

¾ cup white chocolate chips

1. Heat oven to 350°F. Grease 13×9×2-inch baking pan with shortening. Place wire rack on countertop for cooling bars.

2. Combine ¾ cup shortening, brown sugar, granulated sugar, egg, apple butter and milk in large bowl. Beat at medium speed of electric mixer until well blended.

3. Mix flour, baking soda and salt. Mix into creamed mixture at low speed just until blended. Stir in oats, 1 cup at a time, with spoon until blended.

4. Spread half of dough in bottom of prepared pan. Spread raspberry preserves over dough to within ¼ inch of sides. Mix white chocolate chips into remaining dough. Drop by spoonfuls over preserves. Spread evenly.

5. Bake at 350°F for 30 to 35 minutes or until golden brown. (Center will be soft.) *Do not overbake.* Run spatula around edge of pan to loosen before cooling. Cool in pan on wire rack. Cut into 2×1½-inch bars.

Makes 3 dozen bars

Triple Layer Peanut Butter Bars

BASE

1 1/4 cups firmly packed light brown sugar

3/4 cup JIF® Creamy Peanut Butter

1/2 CRISCO® Stick or 1/2 cup CRISCO® all-vegetable shortening
    plus additional for greasing

3 tablespoons milk

1 tablespoon vanilla

1 egg

1 3/4 cups all-purpose flour

3/4 teaspoon baking soda

3/4 teaspoon salt

PEANUT BUTTER LAYER

1 1/2 cups confectioners' sugar

2 tablespoons JIF® Creamy Peanut Butter

1 tablespoon Butter Flavor CRISCO® Stick or 1 tablespoon
    Butter Flavor CRISCO® all-vegetable shortening

3 tablespoons milk

CHOCOLATE GLAZE

2 squares (1 ounce each) unsweetened baking chocolate

2 tablespoons Butter Flavor CRISCO® Stick or 2 tablespoons
    Butter Flavor CRISCO® all-vegetable shortening

1 . Heat oven to 350°F. Grease 13×9-inch baking pan. Place wire rack on countertop for cooling bars.

2. For base, combine brown sugar, 3/4 cup peanut butter, 1/2 cup shortening, 3 tablespoons milk and vanilla in large bowl. Beat at medium speed of electric mixer until well blended. Add egg; beat just until blended.

3. Combine flour, baking soda and salt. Add to shortening mixture; beat at low speed until blended. Press mixture onto bottom of prepared pan.

4. Bake at 350°F for 18 to 20 minutes or until toothpick inserted into center comes out clean. *Do not overbake.* Cool completely on wire rack.

5. For peanut butter layer, place confectioners' sugar, 2 tablespoons peanut butter, 1 tablespoon shortening and 3 tablespoons milk in medium bowl. Beat at low speed of electric mixer until smooth. Spread over cooked and cooled base. Refrigerate 30 minutes.

6. For chocolate glaze, place chocolate and 2 tablespoons shortening in small microwave-safe bowl. Microwave at 50% (MEDIUM) for 1 to 2 minutes or until shiny and soft. Stir until smooth. Cool slightly. Spread over peanut butter layer. Refrigerate about 1 hour or until glaze is set. Cut into 3×1½-inch bars. Let stand 15 to 20 minutes at room temperature before serving. *Makes about 2 dozen bars*

Triple Layer Peanut Butter Bars

Awesome Apricot Oatmeal Bars

$^2/_3$ cup chopped dried apricots

$^2/_3$ cup water

$^1/_2$ cup SMUCKER'S® Apricot Preserves

1 tablespoon granulated sugar

$^1/_2$ teaspoon almond extract

1 Butter Flavor CRISCO® Stick or 1 cup Butter Flavor
     CRISCO® all-vegetable shortening

$1^1/_2$ cups firmly packed light brown sugar

$1^1/_2$ cups all-purpose flour

$1^1/_2$ cups quick oats (not instant or old-fashioned), uncooked

1 teaspoon baking powder

$^1/_2$ teaspoon salt

1. Combine apricots and water in small covered saucepan. Cook on medium heat about 10 minutes. Remove lid. Cook until apricots are tender and water has evaporated. Add preserves, granulated sugar and almond extract. Stir until preserves melt. Cool to room temperature.

2. Heat oven to 350°F. Place wire rack on countertop for cooling bars.

3. Mix 1 cup shortening, brown sugar, flour, oats, baking powder and salt in bowl. Mix at low speed of electric mixer until well blended and crumbly.

4. Press half of mixture in bottom of ungreased 13×9×2-inch baking pan. Spread apricot mixture evenly over crust. Sprinkle remaining crumb mixture over filling. Press down gently.

5. Bake at 350°F for 30 minutes or until crust is golden brown. *Do not overbake.* Remove pan to wire rack. Cool slightly. Run spatula around edge of pan to loosen. Cool completely in pan on wire rack. Cut into 2×1$^1/_2$-inch bars.   *Makes 3 dozen bars*

Top to bottom: Awesome Apricot Oatmeal Bars and Outlandish Oatmeal Bars (page 115)

Nicole's Banana Bars

BASE

> 2 cups firmly packed light brown sugar
>
> 1 Butter Flavor CRISCO® Stick or 1 cup Butter Flavor CRISCO®
> all-vegetable shortening plus additional for greasing
>
> 2 eggs
>
> 1 teaspoon vanilla
>
> 2½ cups all-purpose flour
>
> 1 teaspoon baking soda
>
> ½ teaspoon salt
>
> 3 cups quick oats (not instant or old-fashioned), uncooked

FILLING

> 1 can (14 ounces) sweetened condensed milk (not evaporated
> milk)
>
> 2 ripe bananas, sliced
>
> 2 tablespoons Butter Flavor CRISCO® Stick or 2 tablespoons
> Butter Flavor CRISCO® all-vegetable shortening
>
> 1 teaspoon granulated sugar
>
> 1 teaspoon vanilla
>
> ½ teaspoon salt

1. Heat oven to 350°F. Grease 13×9×2-inch baking pan with shortening. Place wire rack on countertop for cooling bars.

2. For base, combine brown sugar, 1 cup shortening, eggs and vanilla in large bowl. Beat at medium speed of electric mixer until well blended. Stir in flour, baking soda and salt. Stir in oats. Reserve one third of mixture. Press remaining mixture onto bottom of prepared pan.

3. For filling, combine condensed milk, bananas and 2 tablespoons shortening in medium saucepan. Cook and stir constantly on low heat

until mixture thickens and has consistency of pudding. Remove from heat. Stir in sugar, vanilla and salt. Spread over base. Crumble reserved oat mixture over top of filling.

4. Bake at 350°F for 25 minutes or until golden brown. *Do not overbake.* Remove pan to wire rack. Cool. Refrigerate. Cut into 2¼×2-inch bars.

Makes 2 dozen bars

Note: Bars may also be served warm.

Caramel Apple Bars

CRUST

    ¾ Butter Flavor CRISCO® Stick or ¾ cup Butter Flavor CRISCO® all-vegetable shortening plus additional for greasing

    1 cup firmly packed light brown sugar

    1 egg

  1½ cups all-purpose flour

    ½ teaspoon salt

    ½ teaspoon baking soda

  1¾ cups quick oats (not instant or old-fashioned), uncooked

FILLING

    3 to 4 Granny Smith or Golden Delicious apples, peeled and cut into ½-inch dice (about 4 cups)

    2 tablespoons all-purpose flour

    1 teaspoon lemon juice

    1 bag (14 ounces) caramel candy, unwrapped

continued on page 122

Caramel Apple Bars, continued

1. Heat oven to 350°F. Grease 13×9×2-inch baking pan with shortening.

2. For crust, combine $3/4$ cup shortening and brown sugar in large bowl. Beat at medium speed of electric mixer until well blended. Add egg to creamed mixture. Beat until well blended.

3. Combine $1\frac{1}{2}$ cups flour, salt and baking soda. Add to creamed mixture gradually. Add oats. Mix until blended. Reserve $1\frac{1}{4}$ cups mixture for topping. Press remaining mixture into prepared pan.

4. Bake at 350°F for 10 minutes.

5. For filling, toss apples with 2 tablespoons flour and lemon juice. Distribute apple mixture evenly over partially baked crust. Press down lightly.

6. Place caramels in microwave-safe bowl. Microwave at HIGH (100%) for 1 minute. Stir. Repeat until caramels are melted. Drizzle melted caramel evenly over apples. Crumble reserved topping mixture evenly over caramel.

7. Bake at 350°F for 30 to 40 minutes or until apples are tender and top is golden brown. *Do not overbake.* Loosen caramel from sides of pan with knife. Cool completely. Cut into $1\frac{1}{2}$-inch bars. Cover tightly with plastic wrap to store. *Makes about 4 dozen bars*

INDEX

METRIC CONVERSION CHART

VOLUME MEASUREMENTS (dry)

$\frac{1}{8}$ teaspoon = 0.5 mL
$\frac{1}{4}$ teaspoon = 1 mL
$\frac{1}{2}$ teaspoon = 2 mL
$\frac{3}{4}$ teaspoon = 4 mL
1 teaspoon – 5 mL
1 tablespoon = 15 mL
2 tablespoons = 30 mL
$\frac{1}{4}$ cup = 60 mL
$\frac{1}{3}$ cup = 75 mL
$\frac{1}{2}$ cup = 125 mL
$\frac{2}{3}$ cup = 150 mL
$\frac{3}{4}$ cup = 175 mL
1 cup = 250 mL
2 cups = 1 pint = 500 mL
3 cups = 750 mL
4 cups = 1 quart = 1 L

VOLUME MEASUREMENTS (fluid)

1 fluid ounce (2 tablespoons) = 30 mL
4 fluid ounces ($\frac{1}{2}$ cup) = 125 mL
8 fluid ounces (1 cup) = 250 mL
12 fluid ounces (1$\frac{1}{2}$ cups) = 375 mL
16 fluid ounces (2 cups) = 500 mL

WEIGHTS (mass)

$\frac{1}{2}$ ounce = 15 g
1 ounce = 30 g
3 ounces = 90 g
4 ounces = 120 g
8 ounces = 225 g
10 ounces = 285 g
12 ounces = 360 g
16 ounces = 1 pound = 450 g

DIMENSIONS

$\frac{1}{16}$ inch = 2 mm
$\frac{1}{8}$ inch = 3 mm
$\frac{1}{4}$ inch = 6 mm
$\frac{1}{2}$ inch = 1.5 cm
$\frac{3}{4}$ inch = 2 cm
1 inch = 2.5 cm

OVEN TEMPERATURES

250°F = 120°C
275°F = 140°C
300°F = 150°C
325°F = 160°C
350°F = 180°C
375°F = 190°C
400°F = 200°C
425°F = 220°C
450°F = 230°C

BAKING PAN SIZES

Utensil	Size in Inches/Quarts	Metric Volume	Size in Centimeters
Baking or Cake Pan (square or rectangular)	8×8×2	2 L	20×20×5
	9×9×2	2.5 L	23×23×5
	12×8×2	3 L	30×20×5
	13×9×2	3.5 L	33×23×5
Loaf Pan	8×4×3	1.5 L	20×10×7
	9×5×3	2 L	23×13×7
Round Layer Cake Pan	8×1½	1.2 L	20×4
	9×1½	1.5 L	23×4
Pie Plate	8×1¼	750 mL	20×3
	9×1¼	1 L	23×3
Baking Dish or Casserole	1 quart	1 L	—
	1½ quart	1.5 L	—
	2 quart	2 L	—